My Samsung
Galaxy Note™ II

Craig James Johnston
Guy Hart-Davis

800 East 96th Street,
Indianapolis, Indiana 46240 USA

My Samsung Galaxy Note™ II

Copyright © 2013 by Pearson Education, Inc.

ISBN-13: 978-0-7897-4882-9
ISBN-10: 0-7897-4882-7

Library of Congress Control Number: 2013935190.

Printed in the United States of America

First Printing: May 2013

Trademarks

All terms mentioned in this book that are known to be trademarks or service marks have been appropriately capitalized. Que Publishing cannot attest to the accuracy of this information. Use of a term in this book should not be regarded as affecting the validity of any trademark or service mark.

All Galaxy Note II images are provided by Samsung Electronics America.

Warning and Disclaimer

Every effort has been made to make this book as complete and as accurate as possible, but no warranty or fitness is implied. The information provided is on an "as is" basis. The author and the publisher shall have neither liability nor responsibility to any person or entity with respect to any loss or damages arising from the information contained in this book.

Bulk Sales

Que Publishing offers excellent discounts on this book when ordered in quantity for bulk purchases or special sales. For more information, please contact

U.S. Corporate and Government Sales
1-800-382-3419
corpsales@pearsontechgroup.com

For sales outside of the U.S., please contact

International Sales
international@pearsoned.com

Editor-in-Chief
Greg Wiegand

Acquisitions Editor
Michelle Newcomb

Development Editor
Charlotte Kughen,
The Wordsmithery LLC

Managing Editor
Kristy Hart

Project Editor
Betsy Gratner

Copy Editor
Karen Annett

Indexer
Erika Millen

Proofreader
Kathy Ruiz

Technical Editor
Christian Kenyeres

Editorial Assistant
Cindy Teeters

Book Designer
Anne Jones

Compositor
Trina Wurst,
TnT Design, Inc.

Contents at a Glance

Table of Contents

About the Authors

Craig James Johnston has been involved with technology since his high school days at Glenwood High in Durban, South Africa, when his school was given some Apple][Europluses. From that moment, technology captivated him, and he has owned, supported, evangelized, and written about it.

Craig has been involved in designing and supporting large-scale enterprise networks with integrated email and directory services since 1989. He has held many different IT-related positions in his career ranging from sales support engineer to mobile architect for a 40,000-smartphone infrastructure at a large bank.

In addition to designing and supporting mobile computing environments, Craig cohosts the CrackBerry.com podcast as well as guest hosting on other podcasts, including iPhone and iPad Live podcasts. You can see Craig's previously published work in his books *Professional BlackBerry*, and many books in the *My* series, including *My BlackBerry Curve, My Palm Pre, My Note II One, My DROID* (first and second editions), *My Motorola Atrix 4G, My BlackBerry PlayBook,* and *My HTC EVO 3D.*

Craig also enjoys high-horsepower, high-speed vehicles and tries very hard to keep to the speed limit while driving them.

Originally from Durban, South Africa, Craig has lived in the United Kingdom, the San Francisco Bay Area, and New Jersey, where he now lives with his wife, Karen, and a couple of cats.

Craig would love to hear from you. Feel free to contact Craig about your experiences with *My Samsung Galaxy Note II* at http://www.CraigsBooks.info.

All comments, suggestions, and feedback are welcome, including positive and negative.

Guy Hart-Davis is the author of approximately 100 computer books, including *Kindle Fire Geekery* and *How to Do Everything: Samsung Galaxy Tab.*

Dedication

"We shouldn't be surprised that conditions in the universe are suitable for life, but this is not evidence that the universe was designed to allow for life."
—Stephen Hawking

Acknowledgments

We would like to express our deepest gratitude to the following people on the *My Samsung Galaxy Note II* team who all worked extremely hard on this book:

- Michelle Newcomb, our acquisitions editor, who worked with us to give this project an edge

- Christian Kenyeres, our technical editor, who double-checked our writing to ensure the technical accuracy of this book

- Charlotte Kughen, our developmental editor, who developed the manuscript skillfully

- Karen Annett, who copy-edited the manuscript with a light touch

- Betsy Gratner, who kept the project rolling and on schedule

- TnT Design, who laid out the book beautifully

We Want to Hear from You!

As the reader of this book, *you* are our most important critic and commentator. We value your opinion and want to know what we're doing right, what we could do better, what areas you'd like to see us publish in, and any other words of wisdom you're willing to pass our way.

We welcome your comments. You can email or write to let us know what you did or didn't like about this book—as well as what we can do to make our books better.

Please note that we cannot help you with technical problems related to the topic of this book.

When you write, please be sure to include this book's title and author as well as your name and email address. We will carefully review your comments and share them with the author and editors who worked on the book.

Email: feedback@quepublishing.com

Mail: Que Publishing
           ATTN: Reader Feedback
           800 East 96th Street
           Indianapolis, IN 46240 USA

Reader Services

Visit our website and register this book at quepublishing.com/register for convenient access to any updates, downloads, or errata that might be available for this book.

In this chapter, you become familiar with the external features of the Galaxy Note II and the basics of getting started with the Android operating system. Topics include the following:

→ Getting to know your Galaxy Note II's external features
→ Getting to know your Galaxy Note II's S Pen (Stylus)
→ Learning the fundamentals of Android 4.1 (Jelly Bean) and TouchWiz
→ Setting up your Galaxy Note II for the first time
→ Installing desktop synchronization software

Prologue

Getting to Know Your Galaxy Note II

Let's start by getting to know more about your Galaxy Note II by examing the external features, device features, and how the Android 4.1 operating system works.

In addition to Android 4.1 (Jelly Bean), this chapter covers the Samsung TouchWiz interface, which is overlaid on top of Android to adjust the way things look and function.

Your Galaxy Note II's External Features

Becoming familiar with the external features of your Galaxy Note II is a good place to start because you will be using them often. This section covers some of the technical specifications of your Galaxy Note II, including the touchscreen, camera, and S Pen. There are many versions of the Samsung Galaxy Note II, but no matter which one you own or which wireless carrier you use to connect it, the exterior, functionality, and look and feel of the interface are exactly the same.

Front

Indicator light

Proximity sensor

Front camera

Light sensor

Touchscreen

Home button

Menu button

Back button

- **Proximity sensor**—Detects when you place your Galaxy Note II against your head to talk, which causes it to turn off the screen so that your ear doesn't inadvertently activate things on the screen.

- **Light sensor**—Adjusts the brightness of your Galaxy Note II's screen based on the brightness of the ambient light.

- **Earpiece**—The part you hold against your ear while on a call.

- **Indicator light**—Indicates new events (such as missed calls, new Facebook messages, or new emails).

- **Front camera**—1.9-megapixel front-facing camera that can be used for video chat, taking self-portraits, and even unlocking your Galaxy Note II using your face.

- **Touchscreen**—The Galaxy Note II has a 5.5" 720×1280 pixel Super AMOLED HD (Super Active-Matrix Organic Light-Emitting Diode) S-Stripe RGB screen that incorporates capacitive touch.

- **Back button**—Touch to go back one screen when using an application or menu. This is a touch-sensitive button.

- **Menu button**—Touch to see a context-aware menu of options based on the screen or app you are using.

- **Home button**—Press to go to the Home screen. The application that you are using continues to run in the background. Press and hold to see a list of recently used apps and switch between them. This is a physical button.

Back

Back cover removal point

LED camera flash

Rear camera

Volume up/down buttons

Power button

Speaker

- **Volume up/down buttons**—Enables you to control the audio volume on calls and while playing audio and video.

- **Power button**—Allows you to wake up your Galaxy Note II by pressing once. Press and hold for one second to reveal a menu of choices. The choices enable you to put your Galaxy Note II into Silent mode, Airplane mode, or power it off completely.

- **Rear camera**—8-megapixel camera with autofocus that takes clear pictures close-up or far away.

- **LED (light-emitting diode) camera flash**—Helps to illuminate the surroundings when taking pictures in low light.

- **Speaker**—Produces audio when speakerphone is in use. Place your Galaxy Note II on a hard surface for the best audio reflection.

- **Back cover removal point**—Allows you to remove the back cover. Insert your fingernail and pull to remove the back cover. After you have removed the back cover, you can install or swap SIM cards, and insert or swap the Micro-SD memory card.

Top   Bottom

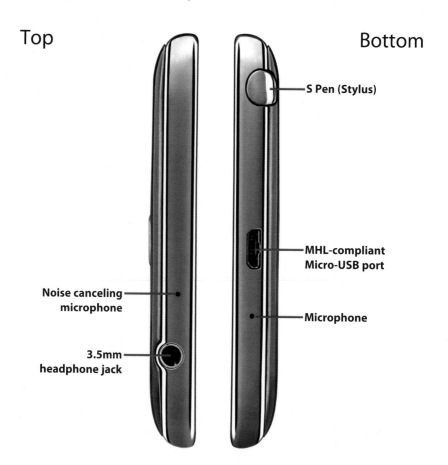

S Pen (Stylus)

MHL-compliant
Micro-USB port

Noise canceling
microphone

Microphone

3.5mm
headphone jack

- **3.5mm headphone jack**—Plug in your Galaxy Note II or third-party headsets to enjoy music and talk on the phone.

- **Noise canceling microphone**—Used in conjuction with the regular microphone on phone calls to reduce background noise. This microphone is also used when you record videos.

- **MHL-compliant Micro-USB port**—You can use the Micro-USB port to synchronize your Galaxy Note II to your desktop computer and charge it, but because it is Mobile High-definition Link (MHL) compliant, you can use it to play movies on your TV via high-definition multimedia interface (HDMI) using a special cable or dock.

- **Microphone**—You use the microphone when you are on a call and holding your Galaxy Note II to your ear.

- **S Pen (Stylus)**—Pull the S Pen out of its holder to draw on the screen and interact with apps. Read more about the S Pen in the next section.

S Pen

Your Samsung Galaxy Note II comes with a stylus, which Samsung calls the S Pen. The S Pen is stored in the Galaxy Note II on the right side and you pull it out from the lower right. This section covers some of the S Pen's features and functions.

Getting to Know the S Pen

Let's take a look at the S Pen itself and learn about its features.

Stylus tip   **S Pen button**

- **Stylus tip**—The S Pen stylus tip is what makes contact with the screen as you write and draw. The stylus tip is pressure sensitive so it knows how hard or soft you are pressing. This is particularly useful for drawing as pressure translates into line thickness.

- **S Pen button**—The S Pen button adds extra functionality to the S Pen. When you press the button as you drag the pen on the screen, you can perform functions, such as moving between screens, taking screenshots, and even cutting out parts of any screen.

Special S Pen Screen

By default, when you remove the S Pen from your Galaxy Note II, a special S Pen screen displays. On that screen, you see the Create Note widget from the S Note app. If you want, you can remove this widget and place other widgets or app shortcuts that you want to appear when you remove your S Pen.

S Pen screen

Air View

Air View is a feature that shows you a preview of information about an object and enables you to interact with it when you hover the S Pen near the screen over an object that is Air View enabled. Here are some examples of using Air View.

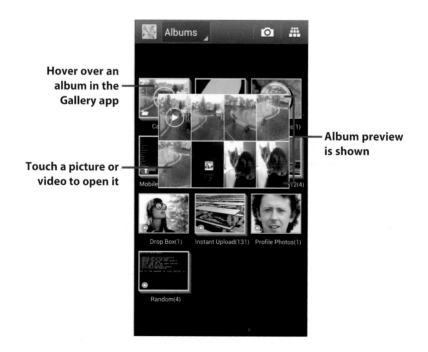

Hover over an album in the Gallery app

Album preview is shown

Touch a picture or video to open it

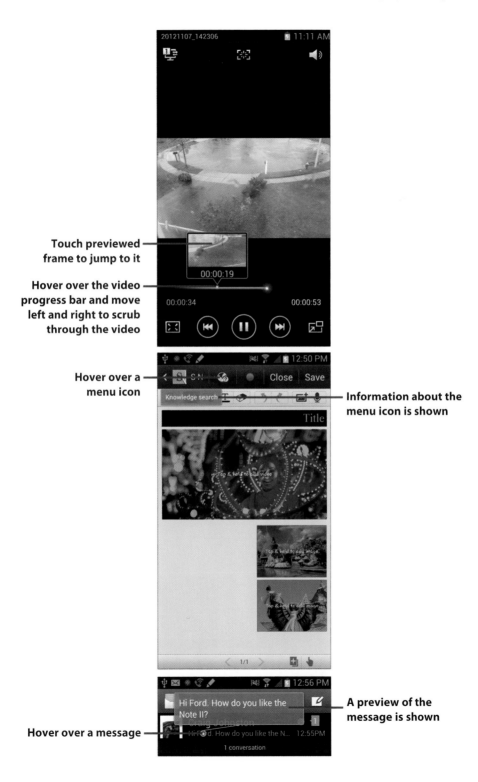

Touch previewed frame to jump to it

Hover over the video progress bar and move left and right to scrub through the video

Hover over a menu icon

Information about the menu icon is shown

A preview of the message is shown

Hover over a message

It's Not All Good

Air View Is Not Always Available

Apps must be specifically written to support Air View, which means that as of the writing of this book there are not very many apps you can use with Air View. For example, although you can use Air View to preview emails in the Email app (which is written by Samsung), Air View does not work in Gmail. Air View is also a little buggy because it sometimes does not work. For example, Air View is supposed to work in the Contacts app to preview contact information, but it does not. By the time you read this book, some updates might have addressed the bugginess of Air View, and vendors like Google might have updated their apps to add support for Air View.

Gestures

While holding the S Pen button, you can draw symbols on the screen to take actions such as going back to the previous screen or bringing up the menu. Here are some examples.

Back gesture

Menu gesture

Double-tap to create a new S Note

Press and hold to take a screenshot

Scrolling Using the S Pen

You can scroll up and down by hovering your S Pen at the top or bottom of an area of the screen that scrolls, such as a message list. For this gesture, you must not press the S Pen button—just hover at the top or bottom of the scroll area. You see an arrow indicating that the scrolling gesture has been recognized.

Hover to scroll up

Draw up to open Quick Commands

Quick Commands

Quick Commands is a feature that enables you to draw symbols on the screen that cause apps to load or activate certain device features. You can even create your own Quick Command symbols.

1. While pressing the S Pen button, draw up from the bottom of the screen to activate Quick Commands.

2. Release the S Pen button.

3. Draw a Quick Command symbol. This example uses the symbol for composing a text message.

4. Write a keyword, such as a name, search term, or place, after the Quick Command symbol. In this example, we want to compose a text message to Craig so we write Craig.

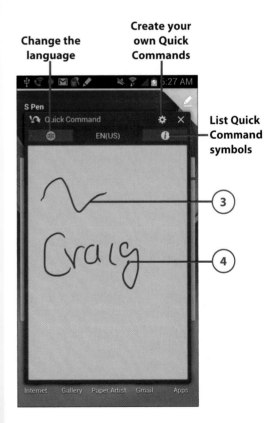

Change the language

Create your own Quick Commands

List Quick Command symbols

5. The command is executed and you should see the app load and your keyword acted upon. In the example, the Message app opens, and a new message is created for Craig.

Default Quick Commands

When you first use Quick Commands, there are a few preloaded that you can use right away. They include searching the Internet for a search term, composing an email to someone, looking up an address in Google Maps, placing a call to someone, and sending a text message to someone.

Grabbing Part of the Screen

Using your S Pen, you can grab any part of the screen as an image. To do that, simply press and continue holding the S Pen button. Draw around the part of the screen you want to capture. Release the S Pen button and the part of the screen inside the shape you have drawn is copied and placed in the Gallery app in an album called Screenshots. Because it is a regular image at that point, you can edit it or share it with your friends.

Draw around the area you want to capture

First-Time Setup

Before setting up your new Samsung Galaxy Note II, you should have a Google account because your Galaxy Note II running Android is tightly integrated into Google. When you have a Google account, you can store your content in the Google cloud, including any books and music you buy or movies you rent. If you do not already have a Google account, go to https://accounts.google.com on your desktop computer and sign up for one.

1. Touch and hold the Power button until you see the animation start playing.

2. Touch to change your language if needed.

3. Touch Next.

4. Touch a Wi-Fi network to connect. If you'd rather not connect to a Wi-Fi network, touch Skip and continue at step 8.

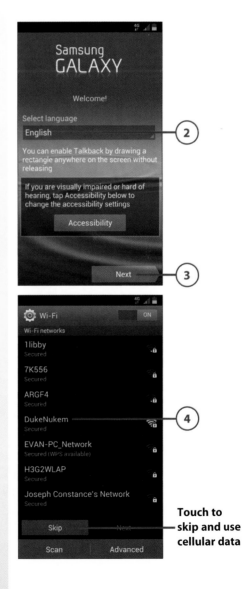

Touch to skip and use cellular data

5. Enter the password for the Wi-Fi network using the onscreen keyboard.

6. Touch Connect. Your Galaxy Note II connects to the Wi-Fi network.

7. Touch Next.

8. Touch to sign in to your Samsung account, if you have one, or touch Skip and jump to step 17.

9. Touch to create a new Samsung account, if you don't have one, or touch Skip and jump to step 17.

Indicates that you are connected to the network

Touch to skip this step

DO I NEED A SAMSUNG ACCOUNT?

>>>Go Further

Android was designed to be used with a Google account. That Google account enables you access to the Google ecosystem of Android apps, music, movies, and books, plus your phone's settings are backed up to the Google cloud. If you change devices, your new device reverts back to the way you had your old device set up. A Samsung account does a similar thing, but it uses the Samsung ecosystem. Technically, you don't really need a Samsung account because Google provides you everything you need. However, Samsung uses the Samsung account to enable certain Samsung-specific features on your Galaxy Note II (and other Samsung Android phones and tablets). These include Group Cast and Share Shot, which both involve sharing content in a group setting.

10. Enter the email address you used for your Samsung account.

11. Enter your Samsung account password.

12. Touch Sign In.

13. Select the information you want to be backed up to the Samsung cloud.

14. Touch OK.

15. Touch to first restore data previously backed up in the Samsung cloud to your Galaxy Note II before continuing.

16. Touch Next.

17. Touch Yes to log in to your Google account.

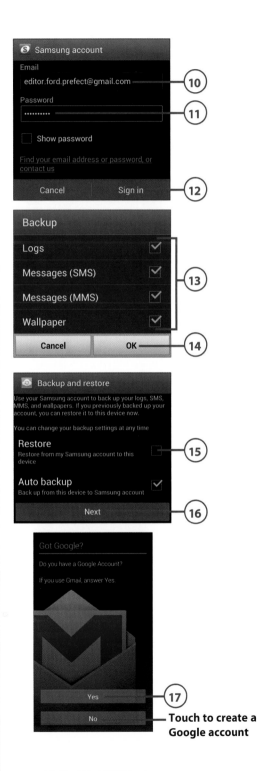

Touch to create a Google account

18. Enter your Google account email address (your Gmail address).

19. Enter your Google account password.

20. Touch to continue.

21. Check this box to restore settings previously saved in the Google cloud to your new Galaxy Note II before continuing.

22. Check this box to keep data on your Galaxy Note II backed up to the Google cloud.

23. Touch to continue.

24. Check this box if you are okay with Google collecting information about your geographic location at any time. Although this information is kept safe, if you are concerned about privacy rights, uncheck this box.

25. Check this box if you are okay with Google using your geographic location for Google searches and other Google services.

26. Touch to continue.

27. Touch to create a Dropbox account.

28. Touch to sign in to your existing Dropbox account.

29. Touch to skip using Dropbox and continue.

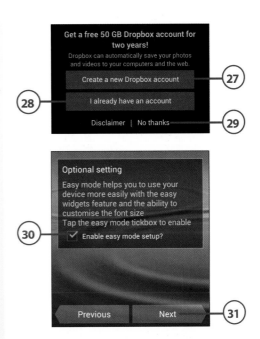

Do I Need Dropbox?

Dropbox is a company that provides cloud storage data. This means that you can use its storage to store your pictures, videos, and other files privately, and choose to share some of that content with your friends. You do not need to use Dropbox on your Galaxy Note II. You can choose other cloud storage companies like Box.net, and even Google's cloud storage.

30. Check the box to enable Easy mode, or leave it unchecked to skip Easy mode.

What Is Easy Mode?

When you enable Easy mode, your Android Home screens are filled with widgets that are meant to help you use your Galaxy Note II. These widgets include Favorite Settings, Favorite Apps, and Favorite Contacts. Later, you can disable Easy mode if you feel it is too intrusive.

31. Touch Next to continue.

32. Touch to choose a different font size for displaying email, contacts, and text messages, or leave it set to Normal.

33. Touch Finish.

Fundamentals of Android 4.1 and TouchWiz

Your Galaxy Note II is run by an operating system called Android. Android was created by Google to run on any smartphone, and your Galaxy Note II uses a version called Android 4.1 (or Jelly Bean). Samsung has made many changes to this version of Android by adding extra components and modifying many standard Android features. They call this customization TouchWiz.

The Unlock Screen

If you haven't used your Galaxy Note II for a while, the screen goes blank to conserve battery power. This task explains how to interact with the Lock screen.

1. Press the Power button or Home button to wake up your Galaxy Note II.

2. Slide your finger across the screen from left to right (or right to left) to unlock your Galaxy Note II.

3. Touch the Missed Calls icon and slide it in any direction to unlock your Galaxy Note II and jump straight to the missed calls list. This icon is visible only when you have missed calls.

4. Touch the Missed Text Messages icon and slide it in any direction to unlock your Galaxy Note II and jump straight to the missed text messages list. This icon is visible only when you have missed text messages.

5. Touch an app icon along the bottom of the screen and slide it up to unlock your Galaxy Note II and launch that app.

Notifications

Working with Notifications and Settings on the Lock Screen

You can work with notifications and set-tings right on the Lock screen. If you see notifications in the Notification bar, pull down the Notification bar to view and clear them. Touching a notification takes you straight to the app that created them. Read more about the Notification bar later in this section.

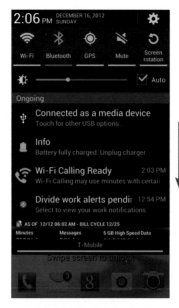

Swipe down to see notifications and settings

Answering a Call from the Lock Screen

If your Galaxy Note II is locked when a call comes in, you have three choices: Drag the green icon to answer the incoming call; drag the red icon to reject the incoming call and send it straight to voice mail; or drag up from the bot-tom of the screen to reject the call and send a preset text message (SMS) to the caller.

Drag to answer

Drag to reject

Slide up to reject and send a text message

The Home Screen(s)

After you unlock your Galaxy Note II, you are presented with the middle Home screen. Your Galaxy Note II has five Home screens. The Home screens contain application shortcuts, a Launcher icon, Notification bar, Shortcuts, Favorites Tray, and widgets.

- **Notification bar**—The Notification bar shows information about Bluetooth, Wi-Fi, and cellular coverage, as well as the battery level and time. The Notification bar also serves as a place where apps can alert or notify you using notification icons.

- **Notification icons**—Notification icons appear in the Notification bar when an app needs to alert or notify you of something. For example, the Phone app can show the Missed Calls icon indicating that you missed a call.

Working with Notifications

To interact with notifications that appear in the Notification bar, place your finger above the top of the screen and drag to pull down the Notification bar and reveal the notifications. Swipe individual notifications off the screen to the left or right to clear them one by one, or touch Clear to clear all of them at once. The Notification bar also includes Quick Settings such as the ability to turn on or off Wi-Fi or Bluetooth.

Touch to go to Settings

Touch to enable or disable a setting

Pull down the Notification bar

Touch to clear all notifications

Touch to launch the associated app

Swipe a notification left or right off the screen to clear it

- **Widget**—Widget are applications that run directly on the Home screens. They are specially designed to provide functionality and real-time information. An example of a widget is one that shows the current weather or provides a search capability. Widgets can be moved and sometimes resized.

- **App shortcut**—When you touch an app shortcut, the associated app launches.

Creating App Shortcuts

Touch the Launcher icon to see all of your apps. Touch and hold on the app you want to make a shortcut for. After the Home screens appear, drag the app shortcut to the location you want the shortcut to be on the Home screen, drag it to an App folder, or drag it left or right off the screen to move between Home screens. Release the icon to place it.

Touch and hold an app icon

Drag between Home screens

Drag to where you want it and release it

• **App folders**—You can group apps together in a folder as a way to organize your apps and declutter your screen.

Creating App Folders

To create a new App folder, touch and hold the first app shortcut you want in your folder. When the Create Folder icon appears, drag the app shortcut to that icon and release it. After you give your App folder a name, the folder displays on your Home screen. Now you can drag other app shortcuts into that folder. To open the folder, touch it to reveal the shortcuts in that folder.

Drag an app shortcut to the Create Folder icon

Give your folder a name

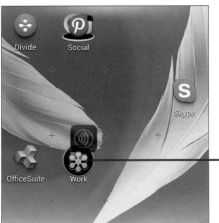

Drag app shortcuts to an existing folder

• **Favorites Tray**—The Favorites Tray is visible on all Home screens. You can drag apps to the Favorites Tray so that they are available no matter which Home screen you are looking at. Apps in the Favorites Tray can be rearranged and removed.

• **Launcher icon**—Touch to show application icons for all applications that you have installed on your Galaxy Note II.

Creating a New Home Screen and Removing an App Shortcut

If you want to create a new Home screen, touch and hold an App Shortcut icon. When the three action icons appear, drag your App Shortcut icon to the Create Page icon, and the shortcut is placed on a brand-new Home Screen page. To remove an App Shortcut icon, drag it to the Remove icon.

Drag App Shortcut icon to Create Page icon to put it on a new Home Screen page

Drag App Shortcut icon to Remove icon to delete it from the Home Screen page

Use the Touchscreen

You interact with your Galaxy Note II mostly by touching the screen, which is known as making gestures on the screen. You can touch, swipe, pinch, double-tap, and type.

 Touch—To start an application, touch its icon. Touch a menu item to select it. Touch the letters of the onscreen keyboard to type.

 Touch and hold—Touch and hold to interact with an object. For example, if you touch and hold a blank area of the Home screen, a menu pops up. If you touch and hold an icon, you can reposition it with your finger.

Drag—Dragging always starts with a touch and hold. For example, if you touch the Notification bar, you can drag it down to read all of the notification messages.

Swipe or slide—Swipe or slide the screen to scroll quickly. To swipe or slide, move your finger across the screen quickly. Be careful not to touch and hold before you swipe or you will reposition something. You can also swipe to clear notifications or close apps when viewing the recent apps.

Double-tap—Double-tapping is like double-clicking a mouse on a desktop computer. Tap the screen twice in quick succession. For example, you can double-tap a web page to zoom in to part of that page.

Pinch—To zoom in and out of images and pages, place your thumb and forefinger on the screen. Pinch them together to zoom out or spread them apart to zoom in (unpinching). Applications like Browser, Gallery, and Maps support pinching.

Rotate the screen—If you rotate your Galaxy Note II from an upright position to being on its left or right side, the screen switches from Portrait view to Landscape view. Most applications honor the screen orientation. The Home screens and Launcher do not.

Use the Keyboard

Your Galaxy Note II has a virtual or onscreen keyboard for those times when you need to enter text. You might be a little wary of a keyboard that has no physical keys, but you will be pleasantly surprised at how well it works.

Some applications automatically show the keyboard when you need to enter text. If the keyboard does not appear, touch the area where you want to type and the keyboard slides up ready for use.

Using the virtual keyboard as you type, your Galaxy Note II makes word suggestions. Think of this as similar to the spell checker you would see in a word processor. Your Galaxy Note II uses a dictionary of words to guess what you are typing. If the word you were going to type is highlighted, touch space or period to select it. If you can see the word in the list but it is not highlighted, touch the word to select it.

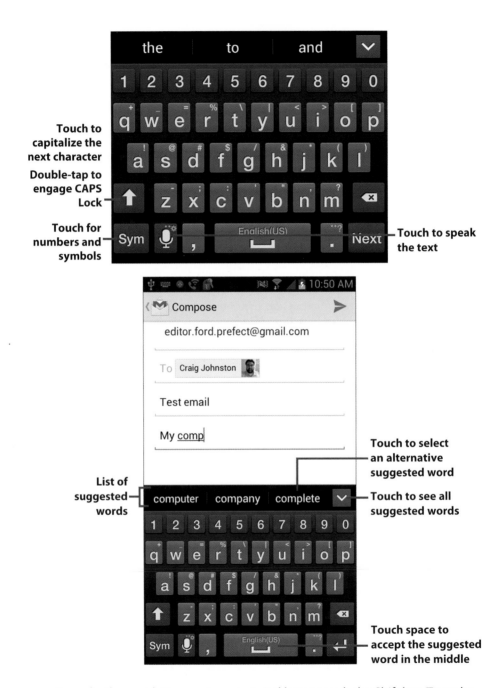

To make the next letter you type a capital letter, touch the Shift key. To make all letters capitals (or CAPS), double-tap the Shift key to engage CAPS Lock. Touch Shift again to disengage CAPS Lock.

To type numbers or symbols, touch the Symbols key.

When on the Numbers and Symbols screen, touch the Symbols key to see extra symbols. There are three screens of symbols. Touch the ABC key to return to the regular keyboard.

Touch to see more symbols —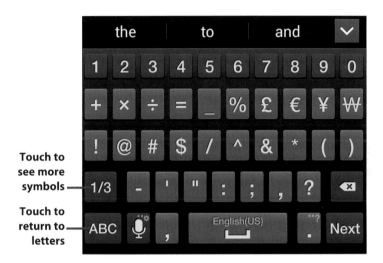

Touch to return to letters

Quick Access to Symbols

If you want to type commonly used symbols, touch and hold the period key. A small window opens with those common symbols. Slide your finger over the symbol you want to type, and lift it to type that symbol.

Select a symbol to type —

Touch and hold to see symbols

To enter an accented character, touch and hold any vowel or C, N, or S keys. A small window opens enabling you to select an accented or alternative character. Slide your finger over the accented character and lift your finger to type it.

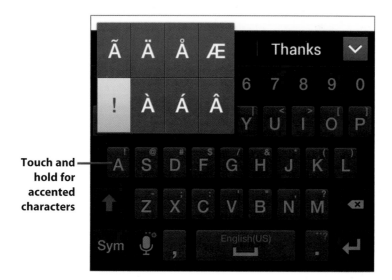

Touch and hold for accented characters

To reveal other alternative characters, touch and hold any other letter, number, or symbol.

Want a Larger Keyboard?

Turn your Galaxy Note II sideways to switch to a landscape keyboard. The landscape keyboard has larger keys and is easier to type on.

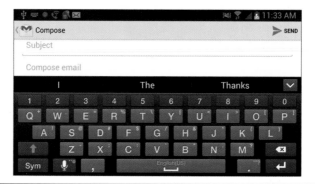

Swipe to Type

Instead of typing on the keyboard in the traditional way by touching each letter individually, you can swipe over the letters in one continuous movement. This is called Continuous Input. It is enabled by default; to use it, just start swiping your finger over the letters of the word you want to type. Lift your finger after each word. No need to worry about spaces because your Galaxy Note II adds them for you. To type a double letter (as in the word pool), loop around that letter on the keyboard.

Dictation—Speak Instead of Type

Your Galaxy Note II can turn your voice into text. It uses Google's speech recognition service, which means that you must have a connection to the cellular network or a Wi-Fi network to use it.

1. Touch the microphone key.

2. Wait until you see Speak Now and start speaking what you want to be typed. You can speak the punctuation by saying "comma," "question mark," "exclamation mark," or "exclamation point."

Touch to select a different dictation language

Edit Text

After you enter text, you can edit it by cutting, copying, or pasting the text. This task describes how to select and copy text so you can paste over a word with the copied text.

1. While you are typing, touch and hold a word you want to copy.

2. Slide the blue end markers until you have selected all of the text you want to copy.

3. Touch to copy the text.

4. Touch and hold the word you want to paste over.

5. Touch to paste what you copied earlier.

Placing a Cursor

You can also simply place a cursor on the screen and move it around to do manual text editing, such as backspace to delete letters or manually insert a new word. To do this, tap on the screen in the text area. A single blue marker displays; drag that marker to the point in the text you want to make changes to. Now start typing or tap backspace, and the action occurs at the cursor position.

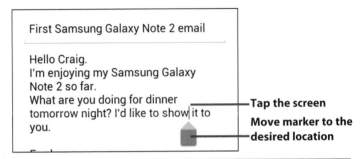

First Samsung Galaxy Note 2 email

Hello Craig.
I'm enjoying my Samsung Galaxy
Note 2 so far.
What are you doing for dinner ————**Tap the screen**
tomorrow night? I'd like to show it to
you.   **Move marker to the**
                                        desired location

Writing Instead of Typing

As discussed earlier in this chapter, your Galaxy Note II comes with the S Pen stylus. Instead of typing on the keyboard, you can use handwriting recognition to write. To enable Handwriting mode, pull out the S Pen from its holder and then touch and hold the Microphone button. Touch the Handwriting icon to enable Handwriting mode. Now write on the screen.

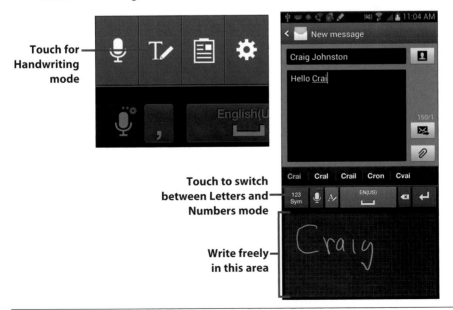

**Touch for
Handwriting
mode**

**Touch to switch
between Letters and
Numbers mode**

**Write freely
in this area**

ONE-HANDED TYPING

>>>Go Further

Your Galaxy Note II is a pretty large phone and unlike smaller phones that have 4-inch screens, you cannot type with one hand on your Galaxy Note II. Samsung addresses this by enabling you to put the keyboard into one-handed typing mode. This mode squashes the keyboard to the left or right of the screen so that you can type with one thumb. To enable one-handed mode, touch and hold the Microphone button and then touch the Settings icon (the cog). Check the box next to One-Handed Operation. Touch the Back key to return to your keyboard, and you'll see that it is now in one-handed mode. Touch the arrow to switch between left-handed and right-handed modes.

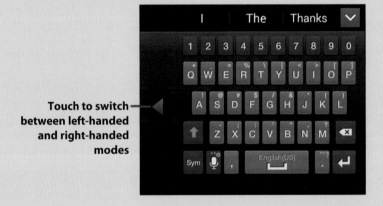

Touch to switch between left-handed and right-handed modes

Menus

Your Galaxy Note II has two types of menus: app menus and context menus. All applications use an app menu. To see the an app menu, touch the physical Menu button, which is to the left of the Home button.

A context menu applies to an item on the screen. If you touch and hold something on the screen (in this example, a link on a web page), a context menu appears. The items on the context menu differ based on the type of object you touched.

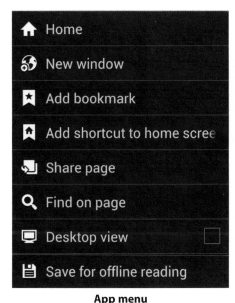

App menu

Touch and hold a link to reveal the link context menu

Touch an item in the menu

Run Two Apps at the Same Time

Your Galaxy Note II has a feature called Multi Window that allows certain apps to run on the same screen at the same time.

1. Press and hold the Back button.

2. Drag an app onto the screen but keep holding it.

Not All Apps Support Multi Window

When you touch Edit to add more apps to the list of Multi Window apps, remember that apps must be specially written to take advantage of Multi Window mode. This means that you might not see the apps you are looking for until the developer updates the app to support Samsung's Multi Window mode.

Scroll up and down to see all apps

Add more apps to the list

3. Drag the app to either the top or bottom half of the screen and release it.

4. Drag the bar up or down to give more or less room to each app.

5. Touch the bar to reveal the Swap and Full Screen icons.

6. Touch to swap the position of the apps on the screen.

7. Touch to make the selected app full screen.

Touch to see the list of apps again

Switch Between Apps

You can switch between running apps and close apps using the multitasking feature.

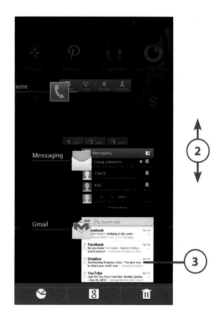

1. Press and hold the Home button.

2. Scroll up and down the list of running apps.

3. Touch an app to switch to it.

4. Swipe an app left or right off the screen to close it.

Installing Synchronization Software

Because your Galaxy Note II is tightly integrated with Google and its services, all media that you purchase on your phone is stored in the Google cloud and accessible anywhere, anytime. However, you might have a lot of music on your computer and need to copy that to your Google cloud. To do that, you need to install the Google Music Manager software or the Android File Transfer app for your Mac to copy any file back and forth.

Install Android File Transfer (Apple Mac OS X)

You only need the Android File Transfer app when using a Samsung Android phone (like your Galaxy Note II) on an Apple Mac running OS X.

1. From your Mac, browse to http://www.android.com/filetransfer/ and download the Android File Transfer app.

2. Click the Downloads icon.

3. Double-click the app in your Safari Downloads.

4. Drag the green Android to the Applications shortcut to install the app.

Install Google Music Manager (Apple Mac)

Don't install Google Music Manager unless you plan to upload files from your computer to the Google Music cloud.

1. Visit https://music.google.com/music/listen#manager_pl from your desktop web browser and log in to your Google account if you're prompted.

2. Click to download Music Manager.

3. Click the Downloads icon.

4. Double-click the app in your Safari Downloads.

5. Drag the Music Manager icon to the Applications shortcut to install the app.

6. Double-click the Music Manager icon in the Applications folder.

7. Skip to the "Configure Music Manager" section to complete the installation.

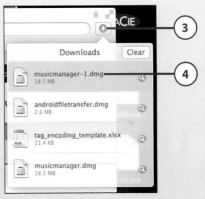

Install Google Music Manager (Windows)

Don't install Google Music Manager unless you plan to upload files from your computer to the Google Music cloud.

1. Visit https://music.google.com/music/listen#manager_pl from your desktop web browser and log in to your Google account if you're prompted.

2. Click to download Music Manager.

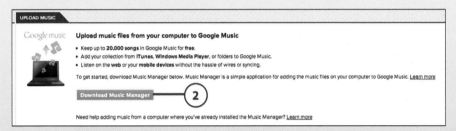

3. Double-click the app in your Downloads folder.

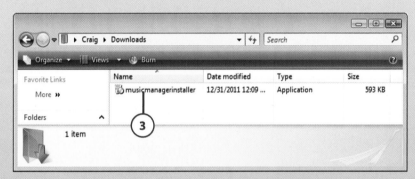

4. Skip to the "Configure Music Manager" section to complete the installation.

Configure Music Manager (Windows and Apple Mac)

1. Click Continue.

2. Enter your Google (Gmail) email address.

3. Enter your Google (Gmail) password.

4. Click Continue.

5. Choose where you keep your music.

6. Click Continue.

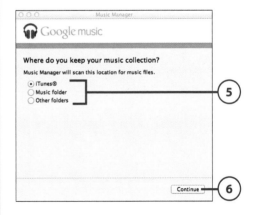

7. Choose whether to upload all of your music or just some of your playlists. Remember that you can only upload 20,000 songs for free. Skip to step 12 if you chose to upload all music.

8. Check if you want to also upload podcasts.

9. Click Continue.

10. Select one or more playlists of music.

11. Click Continue.

12. Choose whether you want to automatically upload any new music that is added to your computer.

13. Click Continue.

14. Click Close.

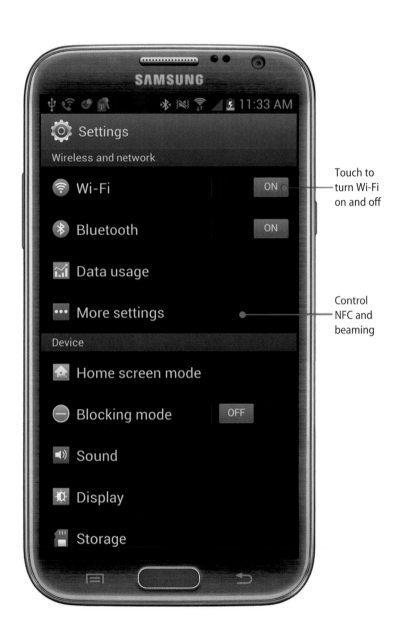

Touch to turn Wi-Fi on and off

Control NFC and beaming

In this chapter, you discover your Galaxy Note II's connectivity capabilities, including Bluetooth, Wi-Fi, VPN, and NFC. Topics include the following:

→ Pairing with Bluetooth devices
→ Connecting to Wi-Fi networks
→ Working with virtual private networks (VPN)
→ Using your Galaxy Note II as a Wi-Fi hotspot
→ Using Near Field Communications (NFC) and beaming

Connecting to Bluetooth, Wi-Fi, and VPNs

Your Galaxy Note II can connect to Bluetooth devices, such as headsets, computers, and car in-dash systems, as well as to Wi-Fi networks, and 2G, 3G, and 4G cellular networks. It has all the connectivity you should expect on a great smartphone. Your Galaxy Note II can also connect to virtual private networks (VPNs) for access to secure networks. Your Galaxy Note II can even share its cellular data connection with other devices over Wi-Fi.

Connecting to Bluetooth Devices

Bluetooth is a great personal area network (PAN) technology that allows for short-distance wireless access to all sorts of devices, such as headsets, other phones, computers, and even car in-dash systems for hands-free calling. The following tasks walk you through pairing your Galaxy Note II to your device and configuring options.

Pair with a New Bluetooth Device

Before you can take advantage of Bluetooth, you need to connect your Galaxy Note II with that device, which is called pairing. After you pair your Galaxy Note II with a Bluetooth device, the two devices can connect to each other automatically in the future.

Putting the Bluetooth Device into Pairing Mode First

Before you pair a Bluetooth device to your Galaxy Note II, you must first put it into Pairing mode. If you are pairing with a Bluetooth headset, you normally have to hold the button on the headset for a certain period of time. Please consult your Bluetooth device's manual on how to put that device into Pairing mode.

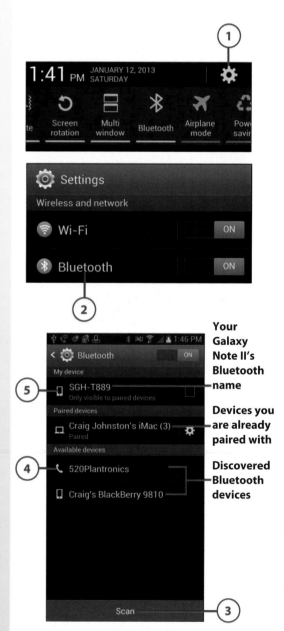

1. Pull down the Notification bar and touch the Settings icon.

2. Touch Bluetooth under the Wireless and Network section.

3. Touch Scan if you don't see the device you want to connect to in the list of discovered devices.

4. Touch the Bluetooth device you want to connect to. In this example, we are going to connect to the 520Plantronics headset.

5. Touch Device Name to change the name that your Galaxy Note II uses when it broadcasts on the Bluetooth network.

Your Galaxy Note II's Bluetooth name

Devices you are already paired with

Discovered Bluetooth devices

6. If all went well, your Galaxy Note
   II should now be paired with the
   new Bluetooth device.

Bluetooth Passkey

If you are pairing with a device that
requires a passkey, such as a car in-dash
system or a computer, the screen shows
a passkey. Make sure the passkey is the
same on your Galaxy Note II and on the
device you are pairing with. Touch Pair on
your Galaxy Note II and confirm the passkey on the device you are pairing with.

All Zeros

If you are pairing with an older
Bluetooth headset, you might be
prompted to enter the passkey. Try
using four zeros; it normally works. If the
zeros don't work, refer to the headset's
manual.

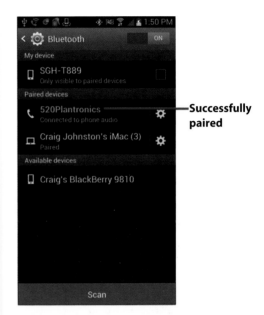

Successfully paired

Touch to confirm the passkey and pair

>>Go Further

REVERSE PAIRING

The steps in this section describe how to pair your Galaxy Note II with a Bluetooth device that is in Pairing mode, listening for an incoming pairing command. You can pair Bluetooth another way in which you put your Galaxy Note II in Discovery mode. To do this, touch the Bluetooth name of your Galaxy Note II on the screen (this is normally an obscure Samsung model number such as "SGH-T889" unless you have changed it). Your Galaxy Note II goes into Pairing mode for two minutes.

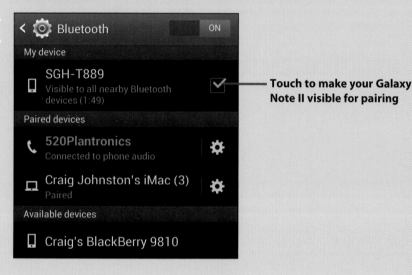

Touch to make your Galaxy Note II visible for pairing

Change Bluetooth Settings

You can change the name your Galaxy Note II uses when pairing over Bluetooth. You can also change the amount of time it remains visible when pairing.

1. Touch the Menu button.

2. Touch to rename your Galaxy Note II phone. You can change it from the obscure Samsung model number to something more friendly like "Craig's Galaxy Note II."

3. Touch to change how long your Galaxy Note II stays visible when pairing.

4. Touch to see any files people have sent you over the Bluetooth network.

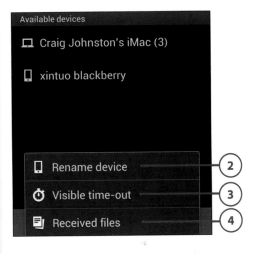

Change Bluetooth Device Options

After a Bluetooth device is paired, you can change a few options for some of them. The number of options depends on the Bluetooth device you are connecting to. Some have more features than others.

1. Touch the Settings icon to the right of the Bluetooth device.

2. Touch to rename the Bluetooth device to something more friendly.

3. Touch to disconnect and unpair the Galaxy Note II from the Bluetooth device. If you do this, you won't be able to use the Bluetooth device again until you redo the pairing as described in the "Pair with a New Bluetooth Device" task.

4. Touch to enable and disable using this device for phone calls. Sometimes Bluetooth devices have more than one profile. You can use this screen to select which ones you want to use.

Bluetooth Profiles

Each Bluetooth device can have one or more Bluetooth profiles. Each Bluetooth profile describes certain features of the device. This tells your Galaxy Note II what it can do when connected to the device. A Bluetooth headset normally only has one profile, such as Phone Audio. This tells your Galaxy Note II that it can only use the device for phone call audio. Some devices might have this profile but also provide other features such as a Phone Book Access profile, which would allow it to synchronize your Galaxy Note II's address book. The latter is typical for car in-dash Bluetooth.

Quick Disconnect

To quickly disconnect from a Bluetooth device, touch the device on the Bluetooth Settings screen and then touch OK.

Wi-Fi

Wi-Fi (Wireless Fidelity) networks are wireless networks that run within free radio bands around the world. Your local coffee shop probably has free Wi-Fi, and so do many other places, such as airports, train stations, malls, and other public areas. Your Galaxy Note II can connect to any Wi-Fi network and provide you higher Internet access speeds than the cellular network.

Connect to Wi-Fi

The following steps explain how to find and connect to Wi-Fi networks. After you have connected your Galaxy Note II to a Wi-Fi network, you automatically are connected to it the next time you are in range of that network.

1. Pull down the Notification bar and touch the Settings icon.

2. Touch Wi-Fi under the Wireless and Network section.

3. Touch to turn Wi-Fi on if the slider is in the off position.

4. Touch the name of the Wi-Fi network you want to connect to. If the network does not use any security, you can skip to step 7.

5. Enter the Wi-Fi network password.

6. Touch to connect to the Wi-Fi network.

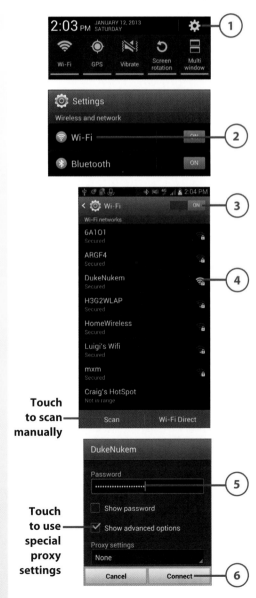

Touch to scan manually

Touch to use special proxy settings

Adding a Hidden Network

If the network you want to connect to is not listed on the screen, it might be purposely hidden. Hidden networks do not broadcast their names (which are known as their service set identifier [SSID]). You need to scroll down to the bottom of the listed Wi-Fi networks and touch Add Wi-Fi Network, type in the SSID, and choose the type of security that the network uses. You need to get this information from the network administrator before you try to connect.

7. If all goes well, you see the Wi-Fi network in the list with the word Connected under it.

Can't Connect to Wi-Fi?

If all does not go well, you might be typing the password or encryption key incorrectly. Verify this with the person who owns the Wi-Fi network. Sometimes there is a lot of radio interference that causes problems. Ask the person who owns the Wi-Fi network to change the channel it operates on and try again.

Wi-Fi Network Options

1. Touch a Wi-Fi network to reveal a pop-up that shows information about your connection to that network.

2. Touch Forget to tell your Galaxy Note II to not connect to this network in the future.

3. Touch and hold on a Wi-Fi network to reveal two actions.

4. Touch to forget the Wi-Fi network and no longer connect to it.

5. Touch to change the Wi-Fi network password or encryption key that your Galaxy Note II uses to connect to the network.

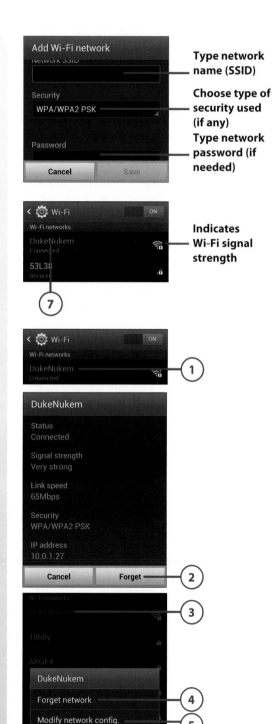

Type network name (SSID)

Choose type of security used (if any)

Type network password (if needed)

Indicates Wi-Fi signal strength

Advanced Wi-Fi Options

Your Galaxy Note II enables you to configure a few advanced Wi-Fi settings that can actually help preserve your battery life.

1. Touch the Menu button.

2. Touch Advanced.

3. Touch to enable or disable the ability for your Galaxy Note II to automatically notify you when it detects a new Wi-Fi network.

4. Touch to change the Wi-Fi sleep policy. This enables you to choose if your Galaxy Note II should keep its connection to Wi-Fi when it goes to sleep.

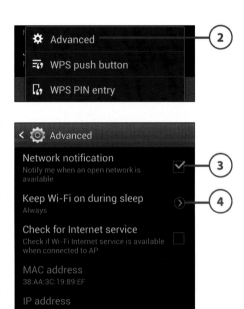

Should You Keep Wi-Fi on During Sleep?

In step 3 of the "Advanced Wi-Fi Options" task, you can choose how your Galaxy Note II handles its connection to Wi-Fi when it goes to sleep. Because Wi-Fi is much faster, more efficient than 3G or 4G, and is free, you should keep this set to Always. However, battery usage can be affected by always being connected to Wi-Fi, so you might want to set this to Only When Pluggd In, which means that if your Galaxy Note II is not charging, and it goes to sleep, it switches to the cellular network for data; when the Galaxy Note II is charging and it goes to sleep it stays connected to Wi-Fi. If you set this setting to Never, it means that when your Galaxy Note II goes to sleep, it switches to using the cellular network for all data. This can lead to more data being used out of your cellular data bundle, which might cost extra, so be careful.

5. Touch to make your Galaxy Note II check to make sure that the Wi-Fi network you connect to has access to the Internet.

6. Use this Wi-Fi MAC address if you need to provide a network administrator with your MAC address in order to be able to use a Wi-Fi network.

7. This shows the IP address that has been assigned to your Galaxy Note II when it connected to the Wi-Fi network.

8. Touch to save your changes and return to the previous screen.

WHAT ARE IP AND MAC ADDRESSES?

A MAC address is a number burned into your Galaxy Note II that identifies its Wi-Fi adapter. This is called the physical layer because it is a physical adapter. An IP address is a secondary way to identify your Galaxy Note II. Unlike a Physical Layer address or MAC address, the IP address can be changed anytime. Modern networks use the IP address when they need to deliver some data to you. Typically when you connect to a network, a device on the network assigns a new IP address. On home networks, this is typically your Wi-Fi router.

Some network administrators use a security feature to limit who can connect to their Wi-Fi network. They set up their network to only allow connections from Wi-Fi devices with specific MAC addresses. If you are trying to connect to such a network, you will have to give the network administrator your MAC address, and he will add it to the allowed list.

Wi-Fi Direct

Wi-Fi Direct is a feature that allows two Android devices running version 4.1 (Jelly Bean) or later to connect to each other using Wi-Fi so they can exchange files. Because Wi-Fi is much faster than Bluetooth, if you are sending large files, using Wi-Fi Direct makes sense. Although Wi-Fi Direct is built into Jelly Bean Android devices, such as your Galaxy Note II, and you can successfully connect to devices, the actual sending of files between them doesn't work. It appears that Google added the functionality, but never extended it to the apps so they can make use of it.

Set Up Wi-Fi Direct

At the time of writing, Wi-Fi Direct doesn't work. If it starts working in the future, use these steps to set it up.

1. Pull down the Notification bar and touch the Settings icon.

2. Touch Wi-Fi under the Wireless and Network section.

3. Touch Wi-Fi Direct.

4. Touch the Menu button.

5. Touch Rename Device to rename your Galaxy Note II from its generic name to something more meaningful.

6. Type a new name for your Galaxy Note II as it will appear to others using Wi-Fi Direct.

7. Touch OK.

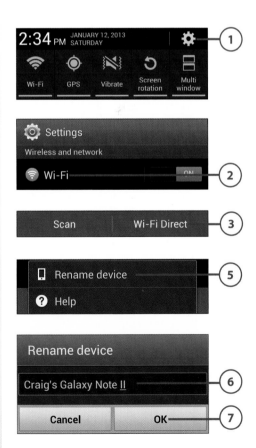

Use Wi-Fi Direct (the Official Way)

Follow these steps to connect two Android devices running version 4.1 (Jelly Bean) or later via Wi-Fi Direct. After they are connected, you should theoretically be able to send files between them, but as of the writing of this book, it does not work. Repeat steps 1 and 2 in the "Set Up Wi-Fi Direct" task if you are not already on the Wi-Fi Direct screen.

1. Ask the other person to enable Wi-Fi Direct on his Android device. After he does, the device should appear on your screen under Available Devices.

2. Touch the device to invite it to connect with your Galaxy Note II via Wi-Fi Direct.

3. Ask the other person to touch Accept on the device you are inviting.

4. The device will show as Connected.

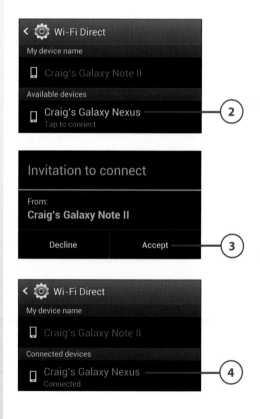

After You Are Connected, Then What?

After you are connected with another device via Wi-Fi Direct, theoretically you should be able to open a picture, video, or music file, touch the Share icon, and share the file via Wi-Fi Direct. When you touch to share it via Wi-Fi Direct, you see a list of devices connected via Wi-Fi Direct. Touch to choose the device you want to share it with. This functionality, however, does not work at all (or at least it didn't during the writing of this book). To use Wi-Fi Direct successfully, you should just use Samsung's S Beam, which uses Near Field Communications (NFC) to set up a Wi-Fi Direct connection between two Samsung phones running Android 4.1 or later. Read more about S Beam later in this chapter.

Touch to share a file via Wi-Fi Direct

Choose the device to share with

Use Wi-Fi Direct (Use WiFi Shoot)

Because the official method of using Wi-Fi Direct doesn't work, you can download an app called WiFi Shoot from Google Play (see Chapter 11, "Working with Android Apps," for more on how to use Google Play). WiFi Shoot, although not perfect, should allow you to send files via Wi-Fi Direct. To use WiFi Shoot, you and the person you want to share files with must both install and open WiFi Shoot.

1. Ask the other person to run WiFi Shoot on her Android device before you start.

2. Find a picture, music file, or video file you want to share and touch the Share icon.

3. Touch WiFi Shoot.

4. Touch the device you want to send the file to.

5. The user of the other device must accept the connection.

6. Touch Shoot to send the file to the other device.

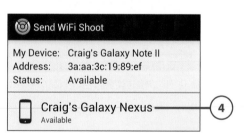

Near Field Communications (NFC)

Your Galaxy Note II has the ability to swap data via its NFC radio with other phones that use NFC or read data that is stored on NFC tags. You can also use NFC to pay for items you have purchased. Android Beam and Samsung S Beam also use NFC to send files between Android devices by setting up the sending process automatically via NFC, and continuing it via Bluetooth or Wi-Fi Direct.

Enable NFC, Android Beam, and S Beam

To get the full benefit from NFC, you need to enable the NFC radio. You should also enable Android Beam and S Beam.

1. Pull down the Notification bar and touch the Settings icon.

2. Touch More Settings in the Wireless and Network section.

3. Touch to enable NFC.

4. Touch to enable S Beam.

5. Touch NFC to see more settings.

6. Touch to enable Android Beam. (See the next section for more about Android Beam.)

7. Touch to save your changes.

>>>Go Further

WHAT IS ANDROID BEAM?

All Android devices running version 4.0 (Ice Cream Sandwich) or later have a feature called Android Beam. This feature sends small bits of data via NFC (such as links to YouTube videos or links to apps in Google Play) to enable you to effectively share content, but it also automates sending actual files (such as pictures and videos) between devices like via Bluetooth.

Use Android Beam to Send Links to Content

You can use Android Beam to send links to content—such as apps, music, and video in the Google Play store or website links—to another device. Android Beam only works between devices that are both running Android 4.0 (Ice Cream Sandwich) or later.

1. Open a website that you'd like to share the link to.

2. Put the back of your Galaxy Note II about 1" from the back of another NFC-enabled phone. You know that the two devices have successfully connected when the web page zooms out.

3. Touch the web page after it zooms out.

4. The browser on the other device opens and immediately loads the link you shared.

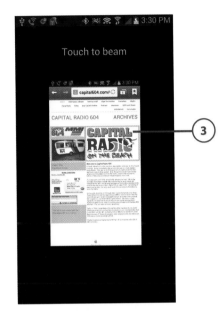

Beam Google Play Content and YouTube Videos

If you like a song, movie, book, or app that is in the Google Play store, you can beam it to someone. Simply open the song, movie, book, or app in Google Play, touch your devices together, and touch to beam. To beam a YouTube video, open the video in the YouTube app, touch the devices together, and touch to beam. The other device opens YouTube and jumps directly to the video.

Use Android Beam to Send Real Files

You can also use Android Beam to send real content such as pictures, music, and video that's stored on your Galaxy Note II. Sending real files using Android Beam only works between devices that are running Android 4.1 (Jelly Bean) or later. This task describes how to beam a picture.

1. Open the picture you want to beam. Note that the picture must reside on your Galaxy Note II and not in the Google Cloud.

2. Put the back of your Galaxy Note II about 1" from the back of another NFC-enabled phone. You know that the two devices have successfully connected when the picture zooms out.

3. Touch the picture after it zooms out.

4. Your Galaxy Note II sends the picture to the other device. The file is sent using Bluetooth in the background.

5. Touch to open the beamed file on the other device after it has been completely received.

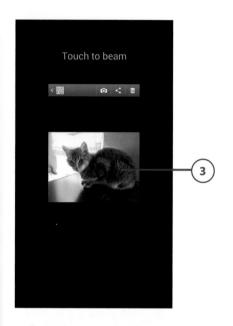

It's Not All Good

Beaming to Non-Samsung Devices

Android Beam is designed to work between any Android devices running version 4.1 (Jelly Bean) or later; however, Samsung included a feature called S Beam that works in a slightly different way to Android Beam. If you want to beam files from your Galaxy Note II to a non-Samsung Android device, you must disable S Beam first. If you don't disable S Beam, your Galaxy Note II simply tries to use S Beam instead of Android Beam, and the beaming fails. You need to reenable S Beam when trying to use S Beam between your Galaxy Note II and another Samsung device.

Use Samsung S Beam to Send Files

Samsung S Beam is Samsung's version of Android Beam, and you can use it to send real content, such as pictures, music, and video, that's stored on your Galaxy Note II. Samsung S Beam only works between Samsung Android devices that also support S Beam. This task describes how to beam a picture.

1. Open the picture you want to send via S Beam. Note that the picture must reside on your Galaxy Note II and not in the Google Cloud.

2. Put the back of your Galaxy Note II about 1" from the back of another S Beam–enabled Samsung device. You know that the two devices have successfully connected when the picture zooms out.

3. Touch the picture after it zooms out.

4. Separate the two devices as instructed on the screen.

5. Your Galaxy Note II sends the picture to the other device. The file is sent using Wi-Fi Direct in the background.

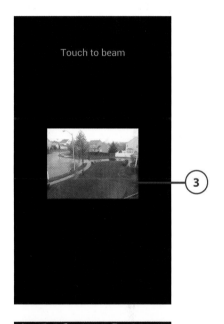

Cellular Networks

Your Galaxy Note II can connect to many different cellular networks around the world. The exact networks that it can connect to are determined by the variant of Galaxy Note II you have because not all carriers use the same technology. To complicate things even more, many devices use different frequencies from one another.

Change Mobile Settings

Your Galaxy Note II has a few options when it comes to connecting to cellular (or mobile) networks.

1. Pull down the Notification bar and touch the Settings icon.

2. Touch More Settings under the Wireless and Network section.

3. Touch Mobile Networks.

4. Touch to enable or disable cellular data. If this option is unchecked, your Galaxy Note II is able to use only Wi-Fi networks for data.

5. Touch to enable or disable cellular data roaming. If this is unchecked, your Galaxy Note II does not attempt to use data while you roam away from your home cellular network.

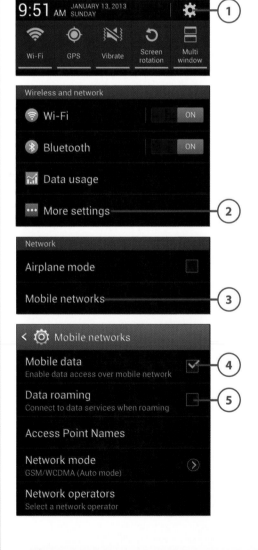

What Is an APN?

APN stands for Access Point Name. You normally don't have to make changes to APNs, but sometimes you need to enter them manually to access certain features. For example, if you need to use tethering, which is where you connect your laptop to your Galaxy Note II and your Galaxy Note II provides Internet connectivity for your laptop, you might be asked by your carrier to use a specific APN. Think of an APN as a gateway to a service.

6. Touch to view, edit, and add APNs. It is unlikely that you need to make any APN changes.

7. Touch to change the network mode. This setting enables you to choose to force your phone to connect to a slower 2G network to save battery or always to a faster 3G or 4G network for the best speed, or to leave it set to Auto mode and let your phone choose for you.

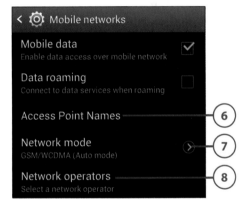

Can I Disable Mobile Data?

If you disable mobile data, you can save on battery life; however, you effectively kill the functionality of any app that needs to be connected all the time, such as instant messaging apps (Yahoo! or Google Talk) or apps like Skype. You also stop receiving email in real time. When this feature is disabled, about 5 minutes after your Galaxy Note II goes to sleep, it disconnects from the mobile data network; however, it remains connected to the mobile voice network.

8. Touch to view and choose mobile operators to use manually.

>>>Go Further

WHY SELECT OPERATORS MANUALLY?

When you are roaming in your home country, your Galaxy Note II automatically selects your home cellular provider. When you are roaming outside your home country, your Galaxy Note II registers on a cellular provider based on its name and how it scores alphabetically. The lowest score always wins. For example, a carrier whose name starts with a number is always chosen over carriers whose names start with letters. A carrier whose name starts with the letter *A* is chosen over a carrier whose name starts with the letter *B*, and so on. As you roam, your home carrier might not have a good roaming relationship with a carrier that your Galaxy Note II has chosen based on its name, so it's better for you to choose the carrier manually to ensure the best roaming rates and, many times, basic connectivity. You will notice that sometimes carriers are represented not by their names but by their operator codes (or Public Land Mobile Network [PLNM] number). For example, 53024 is actually 2Degrees in New Zealand, and 53005 is Telecom New Zealand.

Virtual Private Networks (VPN)

Your Galaxy Note II can connect to virtual private networks (VPNs), which are normally used by companies to provide a secure connection to their inside networks or intranets.

Add a VPN

Before you add a VPN, you must first have all the information needed to set it up on your Galaxy Note II. Speak to your network administrator to get this information ahead of time (and save yourself some frustration). The information you need includes the type of VPN protocol used, the type of encryption used, and the name of the host to which you are connecting.

1. Pull down the Notification bar and touch the Settings icon.

2. Touch More Settings under the Wireless and Network section.

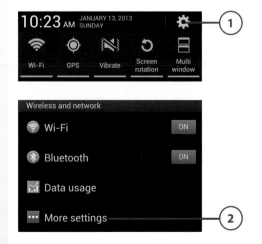

3. Touch VPN.

4. Touch OK to set up a screen lock PIN, pattern, or password. If you already have a screen lock PIN or password, you won't be prompted at this point, and you can proceed to step 6.

Why Do You Need to Set a PIN or Password?

If you don't already have a screen lock PIN, password, or pattern set up before you create your first VPN network connection, you are prompted to create one. This is a security measure that ensures your Galaxy Note II must first be unlocked before anyone can access a stored VPN connection. Because VPN connections are usually used to access company data, this is a good idea.

5. Choose either a pattern, PIN, or password to unlock your Galaxy Note II and follow the steps to create it.

6. Touch Add VPN Network.

7. Enter a name for your VPN network. You can call it anything like Work VPN or the name of the provider like **PublicVPN**.

8. Touch to choose the type of encryption the VPN network uses.

9. Enter the remaining parameters that your network administrator has provided.

10. Touch Save.

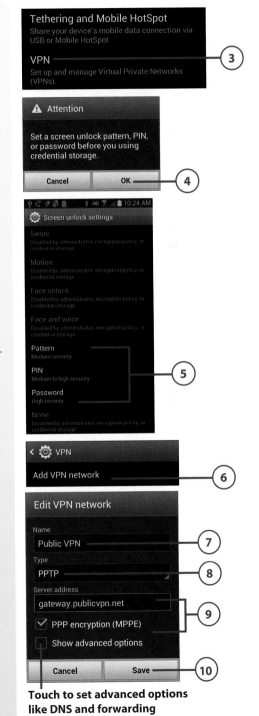

Touch to set advanced options like DNS and forwarding

Connect to a VPN

After you have created one or more VPN connections, you can connect to them when the need arises.

1. Pull down the Notification bar and touch the Settings icon.

2. Touch More Settings under the Wireless and Network section.

3. Touch VPN.

4. Touch a preconfigured VPN connection.

5. Enter the VPN username.

6. Enter the VPN password.

7. Touch Connect. After you're connected to the VPN, you can use your Galaxy Note II's web browser and other applications normally, but you now have access to resources at the other end of the VPN tunnel, such as company web servers or even your company email.

Check to save username and password

HOW CAN YOU TELL IF YOU ARE CONNECTED?

After your Galaxy Note II successfully connects to a VPN network, you see a key icon in the Notification bar. This indicates that you are connected. If you pull down the Notification bar, you can touch the icon to see information about the connection and to disconnect from the VPN.

Connected to VPN

Editing or Deleting a VPN

You can edit an existing VPN or delete it by touching and holding the name of the VPN. A window pops up with a list of options.

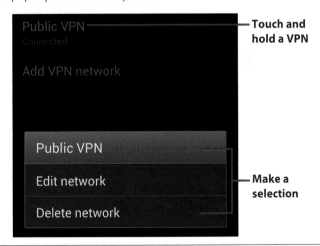

Touch and hold a VPN

Make a selection

>>>Go Further

A MUCH QUICKER WAY TO START A VPN CONNECTION

You can create a shortcut on your Home screen to take you straight to the VPN screen, which cuts down on the steps required to start a VPN. Find the Settings shortcut widget, touch and hold it, and then drag it to the Home screen you'd like it to reside on. When you release it, scroll down and select VPN. Now each time you touch the VPN shortcut on your Home screen, you go directly to the VPN screen where you can launch your VPN connection.

Touch and hold

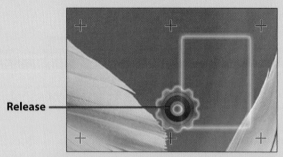

Release

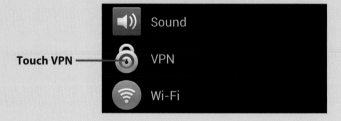

Touch VPN

Mobile Wi-Fi Hotspot

Your Galaxy Note II has the ability to share its cellular data connection with up to eight devices over Wi-Fi. Before you use this feature, you need to normally sign up for a tethering or hotspot plan with your cellular provider, which is normally an extra monthly cost.

Start Your Mobile Wi-Fi Hotspot

1. Pull down the Notification bar and touch the Settings icon.

2. Touch More Settings in the Wireless and Network section.

3. Touch Tethering and Mobile HotSpot.

4. Touch Mobile HotSpot to configure the settings.

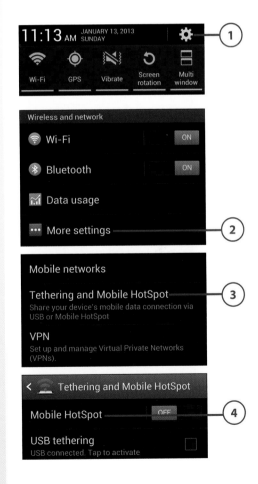

5. Touch to choose whether to allow any device to connect or only devices you allow.

6. Touch Configure.

7. Choose a network name (also known as the SSID) for your mobile hotspot. You can leave it set to the auto-generated name or change it to something more friendly.

8. Touch to enable or disable broadcasting your Wi-Fi HotSpot's network name (also called its SSID). If you choose not to broadcast it, your network will be hidden, but it requires more steps to connect to it.

9. Touch to choose the type of security to use for your mobile hotspot or choose Open to use no security.

10. Enter a password for your portable hotspot if you chose to use a security method in step 9.

11. Touch to change the broadcast channel and maximum connections advanced settings.

12. Touch to save your settings.

13. Touch to enable your portable hotspot.

14. Provide the network connection information to anyone you want to have connecting to your hotspot.

Limit Who Can Connect

People can only connect to your hotspot after you give them the connection information; however, you can further limit who can connect to your hotspot by allowing only certain devices.

1. Touch to add an already connected device to the allowed devices list.

2. Touch to add devices to the allowed list manually.

3. Touch to add a new allowed device using its MAC address. You need to ask the person who owns the device to give you his Wi-Fi MAC address ahead of time.

Touch to edit
the name of an
allowed device

Choose a new
wallpaper

In this chapter, you find out how to customize your Galaxy Note II to suit your needs and lifestyle. Topics include the following:

→ Using wallpapers and live wallpapers
→ Replacing the keyboard
→ Adjusting sound and display settings
→ Setting region and language

2

Customizing Your Galaxy Note II

Your Galaxy Note II arrives preconfigured to appeal to most buyers; however, you might want to change the way some of the features work, or even personalize it to fit your mood or lifestyle. Luckily your Galaxy Note II is customizable.

Changing Your Wallpaper

Your Galaxy Note II comes preloaded with a cool wallpaper. You can install other wallpapers, use live wallpapers that animate, and even use pictures in the Gallery application as your wallpaper.

1. Touch and hold in an open area on the Home screen.

2. Touch Set Wallpaper.

3. Select where you want to change the wallpaper.

4. Touch the type of wallpaper you want to use. Use the steps in one of the following three sections to select your wallpaper.

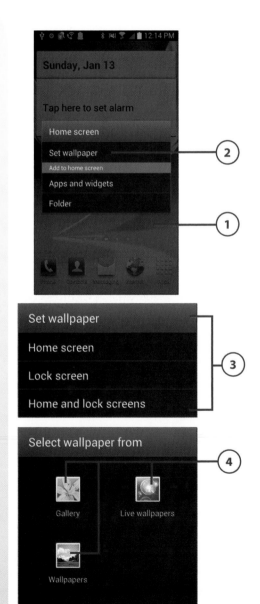

Wallpaper from Gallery Pictures

You can use any picture in your Gallery as a wallpaper.

1. Select the photo you want to use as your wallpaper.

2. Move the crop box to the part of the photo you want to use.

3. Adjust the size of the crop box to include the part of the photo you want.

4. Touch Done to use the cropped portion of the photo as your wallpaper.

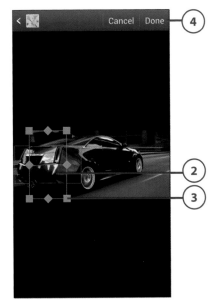

Live Wallpaper

Live wallpaper is wallpaper with some intelligence behind it. It can be a cool animation or even an animation that keys off things such as the music you are playing on your Galaxy Note II, or it can be something simple such as the time. There are some very cool live wallpapers in Google Play that you can install and use.

1. Touch the live wallpaper you want to use. This example uses the Star Trek: Red Alert live wallpaper.

2. Touch to see and change the live wallpaper settings.

3. Touch Set Wallpaper to use the live wallpaper.

Finding More Wallpaper

You can find wallpaper or live wallpaper in Google Play. Open Google Play and search for "wallpaper" or "live wallpaper." Read more on how to use Google Play in Chapter 11, "Working with Android Apps."

Wallpaper

Choose a static wallpaper.

1. Scroll left and right to see all of the wallpapers.

2. Touch a wallpaper to preview it.

3. Touch Set Wallpaper to use the wallpaper.

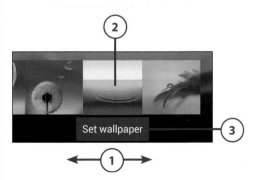

Changing Your Keyboard

If you find it hard to type on the standard Galaxy Note II keyboard, or you just want to make it look better, you can install replacement keyboards. You can download free or purchase replacement keyboards from Google Play. Make sure you install a keyboard before following these steps.

1. Pull down the notification bar and touch the Settings icon.

2. Touch Language and Input.

3. Check the box next to a keyboard you have previously installed from the Google Play store (in this example, we used SwiftKey 3) to make that keyboard available for use.

4. Touch OK to change the input method.

Doing Your Research

When you choose a different keyboard in step 3, the Galaxy Note II gives you a warning telling you that nonstandard keyboards have the potential for capturing everything you type. Do your research on any keyboards before you download and install them.

5. Touch Default to change the default keyboard to the one you have just enabled.

6. Touch the name of your new keyboard to select it to be the default.

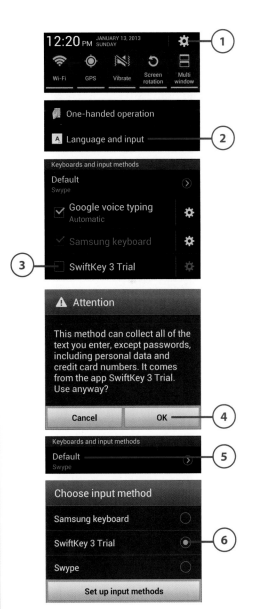

What Can You Do with Your New Keyboard?

Keyboards you buy in Google Play can do many things. They can change the key layout, change the color and style of the keys, offer different methods of text input, and even enable you to use an old T9 predictive input keyboard that you might have become used to when using an old "dumb phone" that only had a numeric keypad.

Adding Widgets to Your Home Screens

Some applications that you install come with widgets that you can place on your Home screens. These widgets normally display real-time information, such as stocks, weather, time, and Facebook feeds. Your Galaxy Note II also comes preinstalled with some widgets. Here is how to add and manage widgets.

Add a Widget

Your Galaxy Note II should come preinstalled with some widgets, but you might also have some extra ones that have been added when you installed other applications. Here is how to add those widgets to your Home screens.

1. Touch the Launcher icon.

2. Touch Widgets.

3. Touch and hold a widget to move it to the Home screen. Keep holding the widget as you move to step 4. This example uses the Dual Clock (Analog).

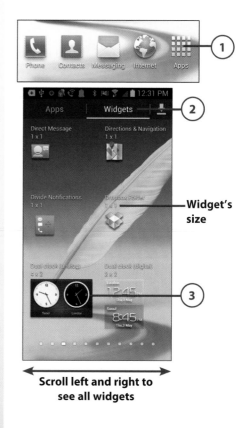

Widget's size

Scroll left and right to see all widgets

4. Position the widget where you want it on the Home screen.

5. Drag the widget between sections of the Home screen.

6. Release your finger to place the widget. Some widgets ask you a few questions after they are positioned.

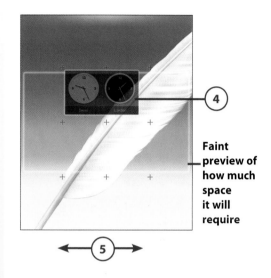

4

Faint preview of how much space it will require

How Many Widgets Can I Fit?

Each part of the Home screen is divided into four blocks across and four blocks down. In the figure for steps 2 and 3, notice that each one shows its size in blocks across and down (such as 1×1). From that, you can judge if a widget is going to fit on the screen you want it to be on, but it also helps you position it in step 3.

5

Resizing Widgets

Some (not all) widgets can be resized. To resize a widget, touch and hold the widget until you see an outline and then release it. If the widget can be resized, you see the resizing borders. Drag them to resize the widget. Touch anywhere on the screen to stop resizing.

SUN
Jan 13

No upcoming calendar events

Drag to resize the widget

Remove and Move a Widget

Sometimes you want to remove a widget, resize it, or move it around.

1. Touch and hold the widget until you see a blue shadow, but continue to hold the widget.
2. Drag the widget to the word Remove to remove it.
3. Drag the widget around the screen or drag it between sections of the Home screen to reposition it.
4. Release the widget.

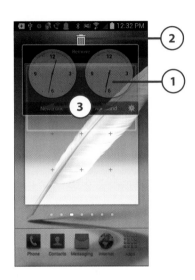

Setting the Language

If you move to another country or want to change the language used by your Galaxy Note II, you can do so with a few touches.

1. Pull down the Notification bar and touch the Settings icon.
2. Touch Language and Input.
3. Touch Language.
4. Touch the language you want to switch to.

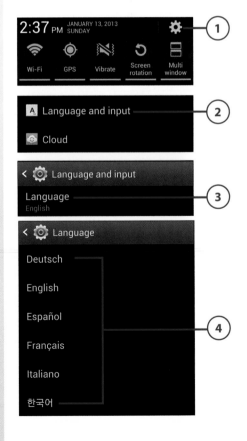

What Obeys the Language Setting?

When you switch your Galaxy Note II to use a different language, you immediately notice that all standard applications and the Galaxy Note II menus switch to the new language. Even some third-party applications honor the language switch. However, many third-party applications ignore the language setting on the Galaxy Note II. So you might open a third-party application and find that all of its menus are still in English.

Changing Accessibility Settings

Your Galaxy Note II includes built-in settings to assist people who might otherwise have difficulty using some features of the device. The Galaxy Note II has the ability to provide alternative feedback, such as vibration and sound. It can even read menu items aloud to you.

1. Pull down the Notification bar and touch the Settings icon.

2. Touch Accessibility.

3. Touch to enable automatic screen rotation. When disabled, the screen does not rotate between Portrait and Landscape modes.

4. Touch to set how many minutes of inactivity your Galaxy Note II waits before timing out the screen.

5. Touch to enable or disable the feature where your tablet speaks your passwords as you type them.

6. Touch to choose whether to use the Home key to answer calls and/or the power key to end calls.

7. Touch to enable or disable the feature where you can press and hold the power key to jump straight to this Accessibility settings screen.

8. Touch to enable or disable TalkBack. When enabled, TalkBack speaks everything, including menus.

9. Scroll down for more settings.

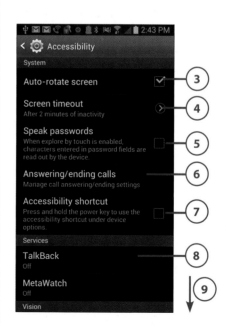

10. Touch to set the font size used on your Galaxy Note II. You can choose sizes ranging from tiny to huge.

11. Touch to enable or disable negative colors where all colors displayed on your Galaxy Note II are reversed.

12. Touch to choose which text-to-speech service to use (Google or Samsung) and rate of the speech.

13. Touch to allow or disallow Google web scripts that make websites more accessible.

14. Touch to adjust the balance of audio played when wearing earphones.

15. Touch to use mono audio when wearing one earphone.

16. Scroll down for more settings.

17. Touch to turn off all sounds.

18. Touch to change how long you have to hold when you perform a touch-and-hold on the screen.

19. Touch to save your settings and return to the previous screen.

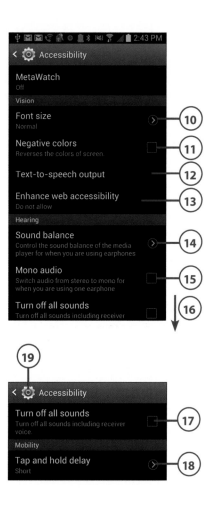

More About Text-to-Speech

By default, your Galaxy Note II uses the Google Text-to-Speech service with an option to use the Samsung service to speak any text that you need to read. You can install other text-to-speech software by searching for them in the Google Play store. After you've installed the software, it shows as a choice in step 12.

Adjusting Sound Settings

You can change the volume for games, ringtones, and alarms, change the default ringtone and notification sound, plus control what system sounds are used.

1. Pull down the Notification bar and touch the Settings icon.

2. Touch Sound.

3. Touch to change the volume for games and media, such as videos and music, ringtones and notifications, and alarms.

4. Touch to choose the intensity of vibrations for incoming calls, notifications, and haptic feedback.

5. Touch to choose the default notification ringtone or add new ones.

6. Touch to choose the vibration pattern used for notifications or create your own.

7. Touch to choose the sound that plays for notifications.

8. Touch to enable or disable playing a sound and vibration when being notified. This option is only available when you have your Galaxy Note II in Sound mode.

9. Touch to enable or disable playing touch-tone sounds when typing numbers on the phone keypad.

10. Touch to enable or disable the touch sounds that play when you touch something on the screen or a menu.

11. Scroll down for more settings.

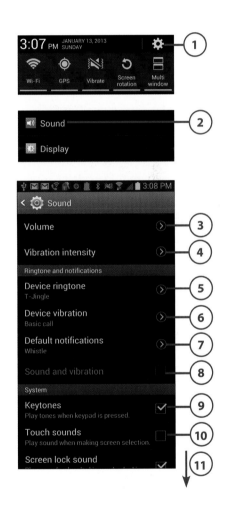

12. Touch to enable or disable the screen lock sound that plays when your Galaxy Note II locks the screen after the inactivity timeout.

13. Touch to enable or disable Haptic feedback, which is a vibration that indicates that you have successfully touched the Menu and Back keys.

14. Touch to save your changes and return to the previous screen.

Creating Your Own Vibration Patterns

In step 6, you can choose the vibration pattern to be used when you are notified, but you can also create your own. Touch Create. On the next screen, touch in the area where it reads "Tap to create," and then tap out your vibration pattern on the screen using short taps for short vibrations and long taps for longer vibrations. The example in the figure uses Morse Code for SOS. You can literally create any vibration pattern you want.

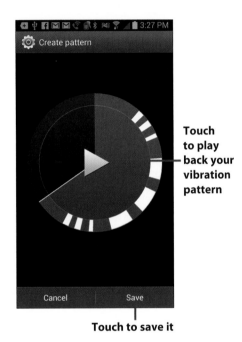

Touch to play back your vibration pattern

Touch to save it

Modifying Display Settings

You can change the screen brightness or set it to automatic, change the wallpaper, change how long to wait before your Galaxy Note II goes to sleep, change the size of the font used, and change whether to use the Pulse notification light.

1. Pull down the Notification bar and touch the Settings icon.

2. Touch Display.

3. Touch to change the wallpaper. Read earlier tasks in this chapter for more about how to change the wallpaper.

4. Touch to choose when the LED indicator is used.

5. Touch to enable or disable Multi Window, which is when two apps run on the screen at the same time. See the Prologue, "Getting to Know Your Galaxy Note II," for more information on Multi Window.

6. Touch to enable or disable Page Buddy. Page Buddy displays a helpful page when it detects that you've done certain things, such as plugging in your headset, plugging your phone into a dock, roaming, or removing the S Pen.

7. Touch to choose which Page Buddy pages are used.

8. Touch to choose the Screen mode, which is how the screen represents colors. You can choose Dynamic, Standard, Natural, or Movie.

9. Touch to change the screen brightness manually or set it to automatic. When on automatic, your Galaxy Note II uses the built-in light sensor to adjust the brightness based on the light levels in the room.

10. Touch to enable or disable Auto-Rotate, which is when your Galaxy Note II uses the accelerometer to detect its orientation and rotate the screen to match it.

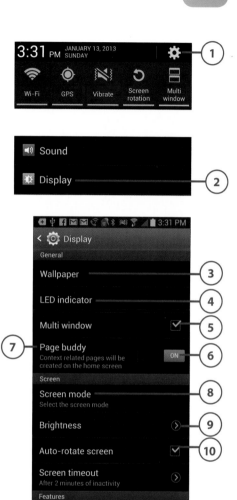

11. Touch to choose how many minutes of inactivity must pass before your Galaxy Note II puts the screen to sleep.

12. Scroll down for more settings.

13. Touch to enable or disable a feature that uses the front-facing camera to determine the orientation of the screen based on the orientation of your face.

14. Touch to enable or disable a feature that uses the front-facing camera to keep the screen turned on while you are looking at your phone no matter what the screen timeout is set to.

15. Touch to choose the font style used for all text.

16. Touch to choose the font size used for all text.

17. Touch to set the key light duration, which is how long the light under the Menu and Back keys remains lit after you have touched them.

18. Touch to enable or disable displaying the battery level as a percentage as well as showing the level graphically.

19. Touch to enable or disable automatically adjusting the tone of the screen based on the kinds of images being shown.

20. Touch to save your changes and return to the previous screen.

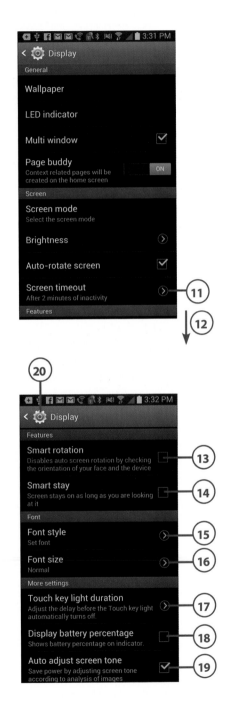

Adjusting Samsung-Specific Settings

On top of the regular Android features, Samsung has added some that only work on their phones. Here is how to set those settings. For this section, assume that all screens start on the Settings screen.

Home Screen Mode

Home Screen mode changes which widgets are placed on your Home screen and how many you have on the Home screen. Easy mode places a lot of widgets that have shortcuts to many apps.

1. Touch Home Screen Mode under the Device section.

2. Touch to choose Basic Mode or Easy Mode.

3. Touch to save your changes and return to the previous screen.

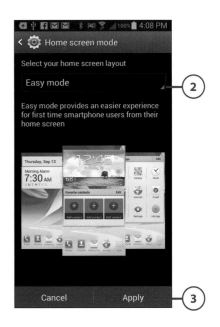

Blocking Mode

Blocking mode enables you to choose a time period when notifications are blocked. This would normally be while you are asleep, but it could be anytime you choose.

1. Touch to enable or disable Blocking Mode.

2. Touch to configure Blocking Mode.

3. Touch to enable or disable blocking all incoming calls while in Blocking mode.

4. Touch to enable or disable blocking all notifications while in Blocking mode.

5. Touch to enable or disable blocking all alarms and timers while in Blocking mode.

6. Touch to enable or disable blocking the LED indicator while in Blocking mode.

7. Touch to set the Blocking mode to Always. Uncheck to set it for a specific period.

8. Set the period of time when Blocking mode is automatically enabled and disabled.

9. Touch to configure which contact's calls will get through when Blocking mode is enabled.

10. Touch to save your changes and return to the previous screen.

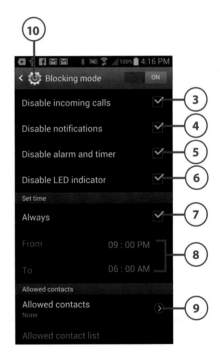

Motion

Motion has a number of features that enable you to use hand movements and phone movements to show information and perform certain functions.

1. Touch to enable or disable Motion.

2. Touch to configure Motion.

3. Touch to enable or disable Quick Glance, which displays key information such as number of missed calls, number of unread emails, and battery percentage if you reach toward your phone while the screen is off.

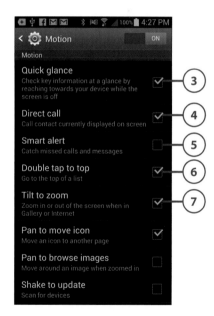

4. Touch to enable or disable Direct Call, which enables you to lift the phone to your ear to automatically place a call to a contact whose phone number is on the screen.

5. Touch to enable or disable Smart Alert, which vibrates the phone as you pick it up if you have missed any calls or messages.

6. Touch to enable or disable Double Tap to Top, which allows some apps to scroll to the top of a list if you double-tap the top of your Galaxy Note II.

7. Touch to enable or disable Tilt to Zoom, which enables you to tilt your phone to zoom in and out of images.

8. Touch to enable or disable Pan to Move Icon. To use this feature, touch and hold an icon to start moving it, and instead of moving it left and right, move the phone left and right to scroll between Home screens.

9. Touch to enable or disable a feature that allows you to move around a zoomed-in image by moving your phone rather than swiping around the image.

10. Touch to enable a feature that enables you to shake your phone to manually update content when in certain apps or settings screens. Examples include checking for new email, scanning for Bluetooth devices, or scanning for Wi-Fi networks.

11. Scroll down for more settings.

12. Touch to enable or disable a feature that mutes your phone when you turn it over.

13. Touch to choose what information is shown when Quick Glance is enabled in step 3.

14. Touch to enable or disable a feature that allows you to take a screenshot by swiping across the screen with the side of your hand.

15. Touch to enable or disable a feature that allows you to mute or pause sounds by covering the screen with your hand.

16. Touch to save your changes and return to the previous screen.

S Pen

The S Pen Settings screen enables you to configure how your S Pen behaves and even makes it possible for your Galaxy Note II to alert you if you leave your S Pen on the desk and walk away.

1. Touch S Pen.

2. Touch to change the dominant hand from left handed to right handed.

3. Touch to change the sound that is played when you detach your S Pen.

4. Touch to enable or disable a feature that opens Popup Note, which is a mini version of S Note, when you detach your S Pen. This can be useful for writing quick notes.

5. Touch to enable or disable S Pen detection, which saves the battery. S Pen detection enables your Galaxy Note II to detect when you remove the S Pen from its holder.

6. Touch to enable or disable S Pen Keeper that alerts you if you leave your S Pen lying around and walk away without it.

7. Touch to enable or disable Air View. See the Prologue to learn more about Air View.

8. Touch to configure which Air View settings are enabled.

9. Touch to enable or disable sound and haptic feedback while using the S Pen.

10. Touch to save your changes and return to the previous screen.

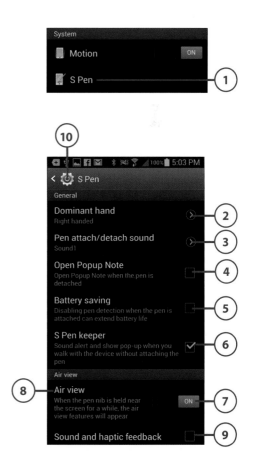

Browse without leaving traces using the Incognito feature

In this chapter, you discover how to browse the World Wide Web using the Chrome browser app that comes with your Galaxy Note II. Topics include the following:

→ Bookmarking websites
→ Using tricks to browse quickly
→ Keeping track of websites you have visited
→ Configuring Chrome to work your way

Browsing the Web

Your Galaxy Note II has a full-featured web browser that enables you to take full advantage of its large screen. You can bookmark sites you want to revisit, hold your Galaxy Note II in landscape orientation so you can see more on the screen, and even share your GPS location with sites.

Navigating with Chrome

The Chrome browser app enables you to access sites quickly, bookmark them for future use, and return instantly to the sites you visit most frequently. You can even sync your open Chrome tabs among your Galaxy Note II, your other portable devices, and your computer.

1. Touch the Chrome icon on the Home screen.

2. Touch to type in a new web address. If the website has moved the previous page up so that the omnibox is hidden, drag the web page down so that the omnibox appears again.

3. Touch to navigate among your tabs. Read more about tabs later in this chapter.

4. Touch a thumbnail to go to one of your Most Visited sites.

5. Touch to display one of the pages you have closed most recently. You might need to scroll down to reach the button for the page you want.

6. Touch to display the list of Most Visited sites.

7. Touch to display your bookmarks.

8. Touch to display your Other Devices list, which shows the tabs open on your other phones, tablets, and computers that use Chrome and sign in to your Google account.

9. Touch the Menu button to display more options for working with Chrome and web pages.

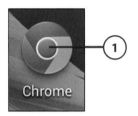

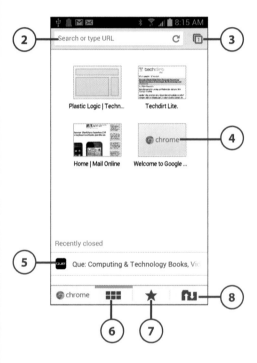

Web Page Options

While a web page is open, you have a number of options, such as creating a bookmark for the page or finding text on the page.

1. Touch the Menu button to display the menu.

2. Touch to go back to the previous web page you visited on this tab.

3. Touch to go forward to the last web page from which you went back on this tab. This button is unavailable until you go back from a page.

4. Touch to add a bookmark for this page.

5. Touch to open a new tab.

6. Touch to open a new Incognito tab for private browsing. Incognito tabs are covered later in this chapter.

7. Touch to display your bookmarks.

8. Touch to display your Other Devices list.

9. Touch to share this web page with other people using apps such as Email, Gmail, Facebook, Messaging, or Twitter. The Share Via dialog shows all the apps you can use to share the web page.

10. Touch to search this page for specific text you type.

11. Touch to enable or disable forcing websites to show the regular view of a web page designed for full-size screens instead of a mobile view designed for small screens.

12. Touch to change the settings for the Chrome browser.

13. Touch to get help.

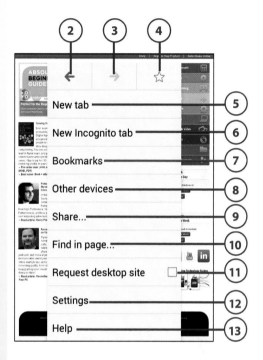

Browser Tricks

The Chrome browser app has some neat tricks to help you browse regular websites comfortably on your Galaxy Note II's screen.

Portrait

1. Rotate your Galaxy Note II so that its long edge is sideways. This puts the screen into what's called *landscape orientation*. Your Galaxy Note II automatically switches the screen to Landscape mode.

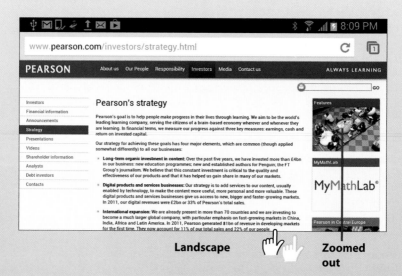

Landscape   **Zoomed out**

2. Double-tap the screen to zoom in and out.

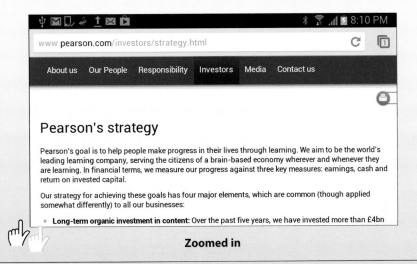

Zoomed in

Pinch to Zoom

When you need to zoom in further, or zoom in to exactly the degree you want, use the alternative way to zoom. Place your thumb and forefinger on the screen and spread them apart to zoom in. Move them back together to zoom out.

Managing Bookmarks, Most Visited, and Other Devices

The Chrome app enables you to bookmark your favorite websites for quick access, but it also keeps a list of the sites you visit most often so you can return to them at the tap of an icon. The app also syncs your open tabs among your devices that run Chrome and sign in to the same Google account, so you can quickly pick up browsing on your Galaxy Note II exactly where you left it on your desktop computer, laptop, or tablet—or vice versa.

Manage Bookmarks

1. Touch the Menu button.

2. Touch Bookmarks. The Mobile Bookmarks folder opens.

3. Touch to display the main Bookmarks folder. From there, you can touch a bookmark it contains or another bookmarks folder.

4. Touch a bookmarks folder to display the bookmarks it contains.

5. Touch a bookmark to display the web page it marks.

6. Touch and hold a bookmark to display a menu of extra actions you can take with it.

7. Touch to open the bookmarked web page in a new tab.

8. Touch to open the bookmark in an Incognito tab.

9. Touch to edit the bookmark.

10. Touch to delete the bookmark.

11. Touch to add the bookmark to your Galaxy Note II's Home screen, where you can quickly access it without having to switch to Chrome first.

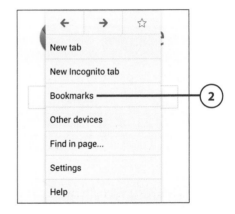

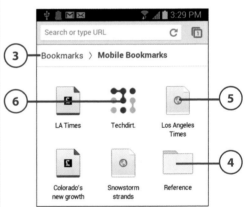

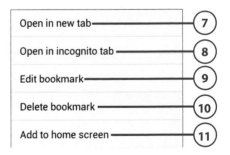

Create a Bookmark

1. Navigate to the page you want to bookmark.

2. Touch the Menu button to open the menu.

3. Touch to start creating a new bookmark.

4. Change the bookmark name if you want to. The default is the web page's title; you might prefer a shorter name.

5. Edit the address if necessary. If you went to the right page in step 1, you do not need to change the address.

6. Select the folder in which to save the bookmark. You can create new folders as needed.

7. Touch Save.

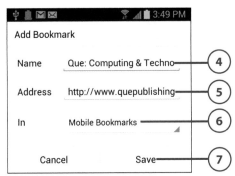

Manage the Most Visited Sites List

The Chrome app's Most Visited sites list enables you to quickly return to sites you visit frequently but that you have not necessarily bookmarked.

1. Touch the Menu button.

2. Touch Bookmarks to display the Bookmarks screen.

3. Touch to display the Most Visited screen.

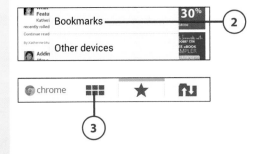

4. Touch to open one of the pages in the current tab.

5. Touch and hold to display further options.

6. Touch to open in a new tab.

7. Touch to open in an Incognito tab.

8. Touch to remove the web page from the Most Visited list.

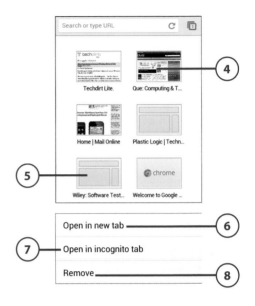

Manage the Other Devices List

The Other Devices list gives you instant access to the tabs open in Chrome on your other devices, such as your tablet and your PC or Mac.

1. Touch the Menu button.

2. Touch Other Devices.

3. Touch a heading to expand or collapse the list of pages on a device.

4. Touch a page to open it.

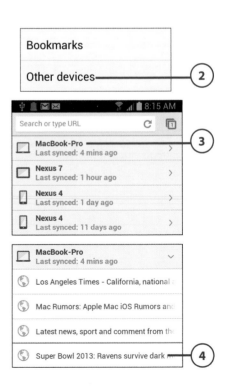

Managing Multiple Tabs

The Chrome app can have multiple web pages open at the same time, each in a different tab. This enables you to open multiple web pages at once and switch between them.

1. Touch the tab icon in the Chrome app.

2. Touch to open a new tab.

3. Touch to close an existing tab.

4. Touch a tab to switch to it.

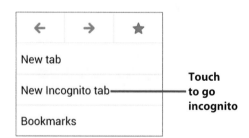

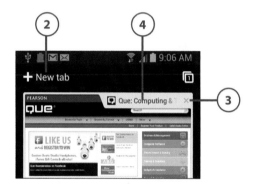

Touch to go incognito

Browsing in Secret

If you want to visit a website in secret, you can. Visiting a website in secret means that the site you visit does not appear in your browser history or search history and does not otherwise leave a trace of itself on your Galaxy Note II. To browse secretly, create a new Incognito browser tab by touching the Menu button and then touching New Incognito Tab. Inside that browser tab, all sites you visit are in secret.

Customizing Browser Settings

You can customize Chrome to make it behave the way you want. Here are the various settings you can change.

1. Touch the Menu button.

2. Touch Settings.

3. Touch your Google account name.

4. Touch to turn sync on or off. If you turn sync on, you can choose which items to sync: bookmarks, omnibox history, open tabs, or everything.

5. Touch to enable or disable sending web pages from your computer to the Chrome app on your Galaxy Note II.

6. Touch to enable or disable automatically signing in to Google sites. Signing in automatically saves you time and typing but decreases your privacy.

7. Touch to return to the Settings screen.

8. Touch to choose your search engine. Your choices are Google, Yahoo!, and Bing.

9. Touch to enable or disable the Autofill Forms feature. This feature lets you add profile information—your name, address, and so on—and credit card information for the Chrome app to fill in automatically on web forms. This means you can complete web forms and spend your money with even less effort.

10. Touch to enable or disable the Chrome app's ability to save your passwords so it can enter them for you.

11. Touch Privacy.

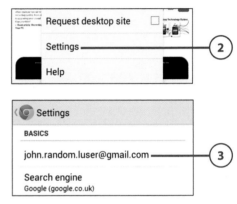

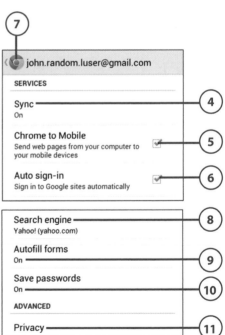

12. Touch to enable or disable showing suggestions for web addresses that you enter incorrectly or that Chrome cannot locate.

13. Touch to enable or disable showing related queries and popular websites similar to those you type in the omnibox.

14. Touch to enable or disable the Network Action Predictions feature. See the nearby sidebar for details.

15. Touch to choose whether to send usage and crash reports to Google. Your choices are Always Send, Only Send on Wi-Fi, and Never Send. If you are happy to provide this data, choosing Only Send on Wi-Fi is usually the best choice because it prevents the reports from consuming your cellular data allowance.

16. Touch to display the Clear Browsing Data dialog.

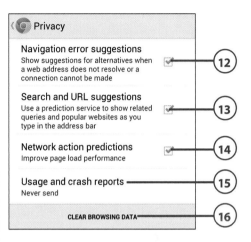

WHAT ARE NETWORK ACTION PREDICTIONS?

>>>Go Further

Network Action Predictions is a feature that allows the Chrome app to preload web pages you are likely to want to load. The app does this in two ways. First, when you start typing an address in the omnibox, the Chrome app preloads a matching web page if it has high confidence that you will want it—for example, because you have visited that page before. Second, when you are on a particular web page, the app might preload the pages whose links you are most likely to click—for example, the top few search results. If Chrome has predicted correctly and loaded the correct pages into memory, when you touch a link, that page renders straight from your Galaxy Note II's memory instead of first loading over the network. Although this can be a time-saver, it means that your Galaxy Note II might preload pages that you will not look at, which can lead to wasted data usage. When you enable Network Action Predictions, you can choose Only Send on Wi-Fi on the Bandwidth Management screen to allow the Chrome app to preload pages only when your Galaxy Note II is connected to Wi-Fi, not when it's connected via a cellular data connection.

17. Touch to enable or disable clearing your browsing history. This clears the history of websites you have visited using the Chrome app on your Galaxy Note II.

18. Touch to enable or disable clearing the cache, data that Chrome stores so that it can redisplay web pages more quickly when you visit them again.

19. Touch to enable or disable clearing your cookies and website data. Browser cookies are used by websites to personalize your visit by storing information specific to you in the cookies.

20. Touch to enable or disable clearing your saved passwords.

21. Touch to enable or disable clearing your Autofill data.

22. Touch to clear the items whose boxes you checked in the Clear Browsing Data dialog.

23. Touch to return to the Settings screen.

24. Touch Accessibility.

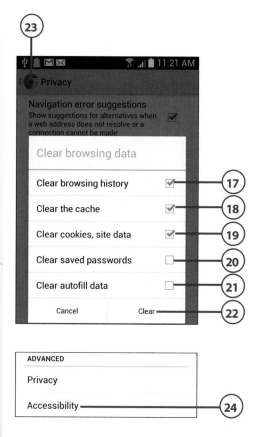

What Is Text Scaling?

When you use text scaling, you instruct your Galaxy Note II to always increase or decrease the font sizes used on a web page by a specific percentage. For example, you can automatically make all text 150% larger than was originally intended.

---

25. Drag to make the text in the Preview box appear at a comfortable size for reading. This is the minimum size to which the Chrome app zooms the text when you double-tap a paragraph.

26. Touch to turn on or off Chrome's ability to zoom in on a website that prevents zooming. Some websites turn off zooming because their creators rate design higher than readability.

27. Touch to return to the Settings screen.

28. Touch Content Settings.

29. Touch to enable or disable accepting cookies. Browser cookies are used by websites to personalize your visit by storing information specific to you in the cookies.

30. Touch to allow or disallow websites access to your GPS information. Providing your location to websites is helpful when you need information related to where you are, but at other times, you might prefer to keep your location private.

31. Touch to enable or disable JavaScript. JavaScript is used on many web pages for formatting and other functions, so you might want to leave this enabled.

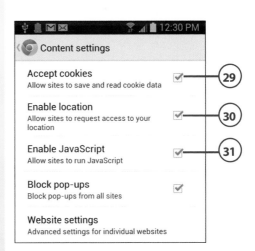

32. Touch to block pop-up windows. Pop-up windows are almost always advertisements, so keeping this enabled is a good idea; however, some websites might not work correctly if pop-up blocking is on.

33. Touch to view the list of websites that are storing data on your Galaxy Note II. You can then clear the data for a specific website if necessary.

34. Touch to return to the Settings screen.

35. Touch Bandwidth Management.

36. Touch Preload Webpages to open the Preload Webpages dialog. (Refer to the "What Are Network Action Predictions" sidebar for more information about preloading webpages.)

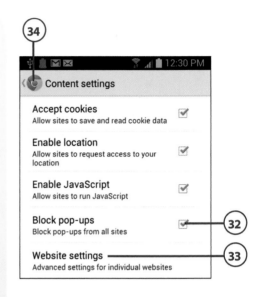

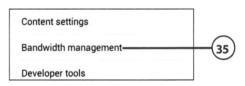

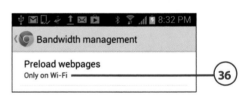

37. Touch to preload pages over both Wi-Fi and cellular connections.

38. Touch to preload pages over Wi-Fi only.

39. Touch to turn off preloading. You would normally do this only if you need to minimize data use on your Wi-Fi connection.

40. Touch to return to the Settings screen.

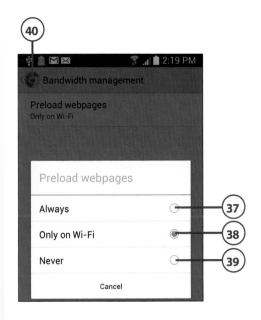

What Are the Developer Tools in Chrome Settings?

The Chrome app's Developer Tools screen offers two features intended for people developing apps for Android, but one of the features is useful for nondevelopers as well. The Enable Tilt Scrolling feature enables you to scroll through your open tabs in Chrome by tilting your Galaxy Note II backward and forward. The Enable USB Web debugging option lets developers use Chrome on a PC or Mac to hunt down bugs in Chrome on Android.

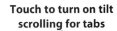

Touch to turn on tilt scrolling for tabs

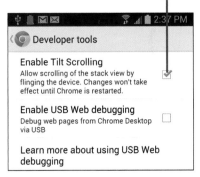

Touch to open email

Touch to open Gmail email only

In this chapter, you discover your Galaxy Note II's email applications for Gmail and other accounts, such as POP3, IMAP, and even Microsoft Exchange. Topics include the following:

→ Sending and receiving email

→ Working with attachments

→ Working with Gmail labels

→ Changing settings

Email

Your Galaxy Note II has two email programs: the Gmail app, which only works with Gmail, and the Email app that works with POP3, IMAP, and Microsoft Exchange accounts.

Gmail

When you first set up your Galaxy Note II, you set up a Gmail account. The Gmail application enables you to have multiple Gmail accounts, which is useful if you have a business account and a personal account.

Add a Google Account

When you first set up your Galaxy Note II, you added your first Google (Gmail) account. The following steps describe how to add a second account.

1. Touch to open the Gmail app.

2. Touch the Menu button.

3. Touch Settings.

4. Touch Add Account.

5. Touch Existing.

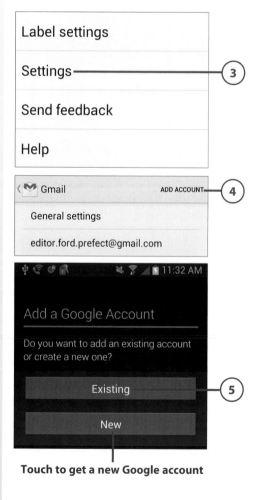

Touch to get a new Google account

6. Enter your existing Google account name. This is your Gmail address.

What If I Don't Have a Second Google Account?

If you don't already have a second Google account but want to set one up, in step 5, touch Get a Google Account. Your Galaxy Note II walks you through the steps of choosing a new Google account.

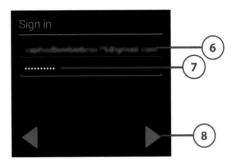

7. Enter your existing Google password.

8. Touch to sign in.

9. Select what components of your Google account you want to synchronize with your Galaxy Note II.

10. Touch to finish the Google account setup.

Why Multiple Google Accounts?

You are probably wondering why you would want multiple Google accounts. Isn't one good enough? Actually, it is not that uncommon to have multiple Google accounts. It can be a way to compartmentalize your life between work and play. You might run a small business using one account, but email only friends with another. Your Galaxy Note II supports multiple accounts, but still enables you to interact with them in one place.

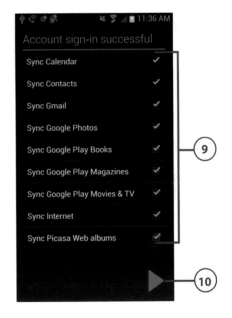

Navigate the Gmail App

This task shows you how to navigate the main screen of the Gmail app.

1. Touch the Gmail icon.

2. Touch to switch between Gmail accounts (if you use more than one) or switch from the Inbox label to one of your other labels.

3. Touch to compose a new email.

4. Touch to search the current label for an email.

5. Touch to manually refresh the current view.

6. Touch to manage your labels.

7. Touch the star to add the email to the Starred label.

Stars and Labels

Gmail allows you to use stars and labels to help organize your email. In most email clients, you can create folders in your mailbox to help you organize your emails. For example, you might create a folder called "emails from the boss" and move any emails you receive to that folder. Gmail doesn't use the term folders; instead, it uses the term labels. You can create labels in Gmail and choose an email to label. When you do this, it actually moves it to a folder with that label, but to you, the email has a label distinguishing it from other emails. And email that you mark with a star is actually just getting a label called "starred." But when viewing your Gmail, you see the yellow star next to an email. People normally add a star to an email as a reminder of something important.

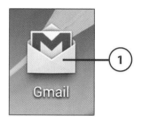

Unread messages

Indicates that the email is important

Compose Gmail Email

1. Touch the Compose icon.

2. Touch to change the Gmail account from which the message is being sent (if you have multiple Gmail accounts).

3. Type names in the To field. If the name matches someone in your Contacts, the name is displayed and you can touch it to select it.

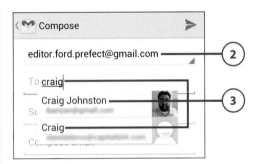

Can You Carbon Copy (Cc) and Blind Carbon Copy(Bcc)?

While you are composing your email, you can add recipients to the To field, as shown in the figure for step 3; however, there are no Carbon Copy (Cc) and Blind Carbon Copy (Bcc) fields shown. You can add these fields by touching the Menu button and touching Add Cc/Bcc. After you do that, the Cc and Bcc fields display.

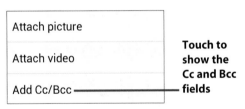

Touch to show the Cc and Bcc fields

4. Type a subject for your email.

5. Type the body of the email.

6. Touch to send the email.

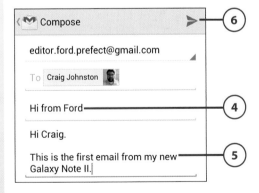

Add Attachments to Messages

Before sending an email, you can add one or more attachments. You can attach pictures or videos, but if you use Dropbox you can attach any file that is in your Dropbox folders. If you use OfficeSuite for your Microsoft Office documents, you can attach files from there, too.

1. With an email message open, touch the Menu button.

2. Touch Attach Picture or Attach Video (they do the same thing).

3. Touch Gallery.

4. Navigate the Gallery app to find the picture you want to attach.

5. Attachments are listed below the body of the email.

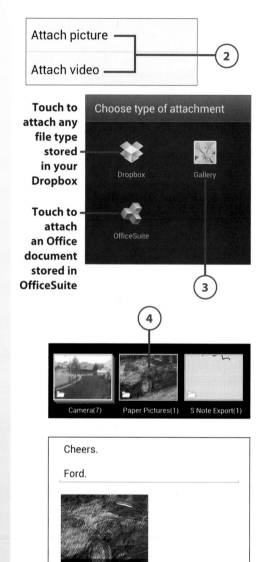

Attach picture

Attach video

2

Touch to attach any file type stored in your Dropbox

Choose type of attachment

Dropbox

Gallery

Touch to attach an Office document stored in OfficeSuite

OfficeSuite

3

4

Camera(7)   Paper Pictures(1)   S Note Export(1)

Cheers.

Ford.

PaperArtist_2
1.9MB Image ✕

📎 Capital radio Intro 1979.mp3   ✕

📎 Craig James Johnston - Mobile.doc   ✕

Touch to remove the attachment

Read Gmail Email

1. Touch an email to open it.

2. Touch to expand the original email, if the email you are reading is a reply.

3. Touch to reply to the sender of the email. This does not reply to anyone in the Cc field.

4. Touch the menu bar to do a Reply All (reply to all recipients) or Forward the email.

5. Touch to expand the email header to see all recipients and all other email header information.

6. Touch to "star" the email, which adds it to the star label. Read more about labels earlier in this chapter.

7. Touch to move the email to the Gmail Archive folder.

8. Touch to permanently delete the email.

9. Touch to change the label of the email. Read more about labels earlier in this chapter.

10. Touch to mark the message as unread and return to the message list.

Indicates attachments

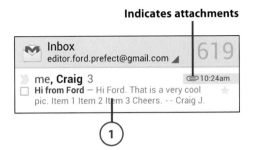

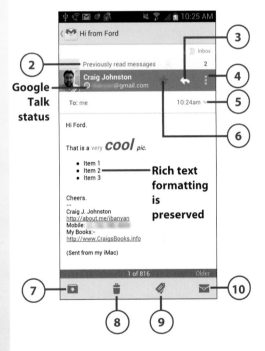

Google Talk status

Rich text formatting is preserved

More Email Actions

1. Touch the Menu button.

2. Touch to report the email as spam.

3. Touch to mute the email conversation. Once muted, you no longer see emails in the conversation.

4. Touch to report the email as a phishing scam.

5. Touch to mark the message as not important or important.

Mark not important	5
Mute	3
Report spam	2
Report phishing	4
Settings	
Send feedback	
Help	

What Is Important?

Gmail tries to automatically figure out which of the emails you receive are important. As it learns, it might guess wrong. If an email is marked as important but it is not important, you can manually change the status to not important as described in step 5. Important emails have a yellow arrow, whereas emails that are not important have a clear arrow.

What Are Conversations?

Conversations are Gmail's version of email threads. When you look at the main view of the Gmail app, you see a list of email conversations. The conversation might have only one email in it, but to Gmail that's a conversation. As you and others reply to that original email, Gmail groups those emails in a thread, or conversation.

What Happens to Your Spam and Phishing Emails?

When you mark an email in Gmail as spam or a phishing scam, two things happen. The message gets a label called Spam. In addition, a copy of that email is sent to Gmail's spam servers so they are now aware of a possible new spam or phishing scam email that is circulating around the Internet. Based on what the servers see for all Gmail users, they block that spam or phishing email from reaching other Gmail users. So the bottom line is that you should always mark spam and phishing emails because it helps all of us.

Modify Gmail Settings

You can customize the way Gmail accounts work on your Galaxy Note II, including changing the email signature and choosing which labels synchronize.

1. Touch the Menu button.

2. Touch Settings.

Email Signature

An email signature is a bit of text that is automatically added to the bottom of any emails you send from your Galaxy Note II. It is added when you compose a new email, reply to an email, or forward an email. A typical use for a signature is to automatically add your name and maybe some contact information at the end of your emails. Email signatures are sometimes referred to as email footers.

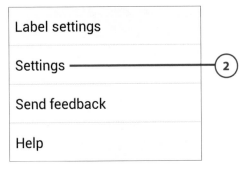

3. Touch General Settings.

4. Touch to enable or disable confirmation before deleting a message or entire conversation.

5. Touch to enable or disable confirmation before archiving a message or entire conversation.

6. Touch to enable or disable confirmation before sending an email.

7. Touch to change what happens if you swipe your finger over a conversation list. You can set it so that nothing happens, the conversation is archived, or it is deleted.

8. Touch to enable or disable making Reply All the default action when replying to emails. Normally only Reply is used. Reply All replies to the sender and all recipients.

9. Touch to enable or disable Auto-fit. When enabled, Auto-fit shrinks all emails so that they fit on the screen, but you can use the unpinch gesture to zoom in.

10. Touch Auto-advance to select which screen your Galaxy Note II must show after you delete or archive an email. Your choices are Newer Conversation, Older Conversation, and Conversation List.

11. Touch to enable or disable hiding the check boxes in the conversation List. When this is not enabled, there are always check boxes next to emails in the conversation list. This enables you to select more than one email and take action on it. If you enable this, the check boxes are hidden, forcing you to touch and hold to select multiple messages.

12. Scroll down for more options.

13. Touch to change the behavior of the blue message actions bar as you scroll through a message. Your choices are to keep it at the top of the screen as you scroll, only keep it at the top of the screen when in Portrait mode, or let it scroll up with the message as you scroll.

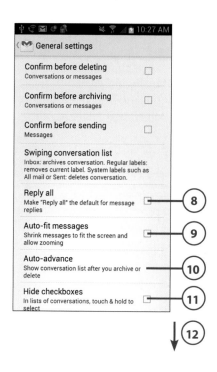

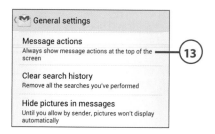

14. Touch to clear the Gmail search history.

15. Touch to restore the setting for whether to automatically load pictures when reading email. By default, this is set to Off.

16. Touch to return to the main Settings screen.

17. Touch one of your Gmail accounts to change settings specific to that account.

18. Touch to enable or disable showing your Priority Inbox instead of your regular Inbox when opening the Gmail app.

19. Touch to enable or disable getting notified when new email arrives for this Gmail account.

20. Touch to select how to get notified when new email arrives for this account.

21. Touch to enter a signature that will appear at the end of all emails composed using this account.

22. Touch to change how this account is synchronized, what is synchronized, or remove it entirely.

23. Touch to select how many days of mail to synchronize with your Galaxy Note II.

24. Touch to manage labels. Read more about managing labels in the next task.

25. Touch to enable or disable downloading attachments while connected to a Wi-Fi network.

26. Touch to return to the main Settings screen.

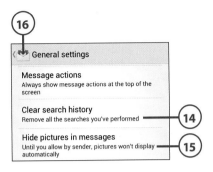

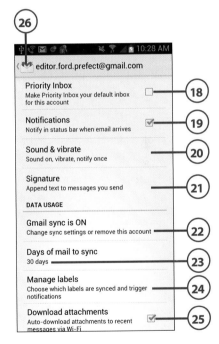

Manage Gmail Labels

Gmail labels are Google's name for email folders. You can manage how each of them synchronize and alert you.

1. Touch the Inbox label.

2. Touch Show All Labels.

3. Touch Manage Labels.

4. Touch a label to manage it.

5. Touch to enable synchronization of this label to your Galaxy Note II and whether to synchronize 30 days of email or all email. After synchronization is enabled, the rest of the settings on this screen become available.

6. Touch to enable or disable being notified when new email arrives in this label.

7. Touch to select the ringtone that plays when you are notified of new email in this label.

8. Touch to choose whether to also vibrate when new email arrives in this label.

9. Touch to enable or disable notifying you once when multiple emails arrive in this label, as opposed to notifying for each one.

10. Touch to return to the list of labels.

Alternatively, you can touch here

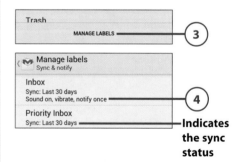

Indicates the sync status

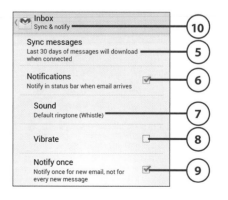

Email Application

The Email application supports all email accounts with the exception of Gmail. This includes any corporate email accounts that use Microsoft Exchange or corporate emails systems such as Lotus Domino/Notes that have an ActiveSync gateway. In addition to corporate email accounts, the Email application also supports POP3 and IMAP accounts. These are typically hosted by your Internet service provider, but also by places like Yahoo! or Hotmail.

Add a Work Email Account

Your Galaxy Note II can synchronize your contacts from your work email account as long as your company uses Microsoft Exchange or an email gateway that supports Microsoft ActiveSync (such as Lotus Traveler for Lotus Domino/Notes email systems). It might be useful to be able to keep your work and personal contacts on one mobile device instead of carrying two phones around all day.

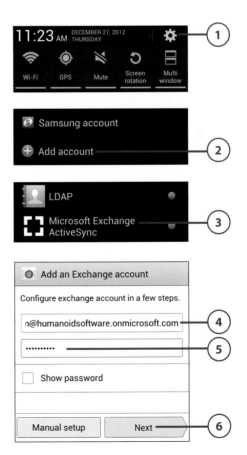

1. From the Home screen, pull down the Notification bar and touch the Settings icon.

2. Scroll down to the Accounts section and touch Add Account.

3. Touch Microsoft Exchange ActiveSync.

4. Enter your full corporate email address.

5. Enter your corporate network password.

6. Touch Next.

7. Enter your company's mail server name.

Error Adding Account? Guess the Server

Your Galaxy Note II tries to work out some information about your company's ActiveSync setup. If it can't, you are prompted to enter the ActiveSync server name manually. If you don't know what it is, you can try guessing it. If, for example, your email address is dsimons@allhitradio.com, the ActiveSync server is most probably webmail.allhitradio.com or autodiscover.allhitradio.com. If this doesn't work, ask your email administrator.

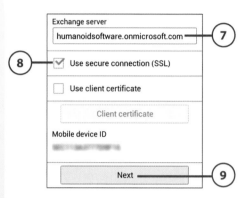

8. Touch to use secure connections, which encrypts your email, calendar, and contacts between your Galaxy Note II and your company's mail server. It is highly recommended that you leave this selected.

9. Touch Next.

10. Touch to agree that your mail administrator may impose security restrictions on your Galaxy Note II if you proceed.

11. Touch to choose how often your corporate email is delivered to your Galaxy Note II. Push means that as it arrives in your Inbox at work, it is delivered to your phone. You can set it to Manual, which means that your work email is only delivered when you open the Email app on your phone. You can also set the delivery frequency from every 5 minutes to every hour.

12. Touch to choose how many days in the past email is synchronized to your Galaxy Note II.

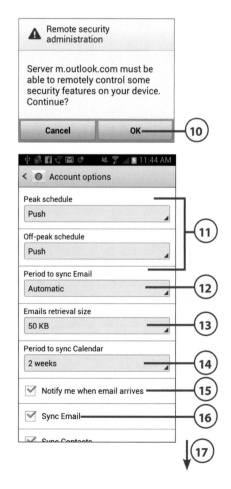

13. Touch to choose how much of an email is retrieved.

14. Touch to choose how many days in the past calendar items are synchronized to your Galaxy Note II.

15. Touch to enable or disable being notified when new email arrives from your corporate Inbox.

16. Touch to enable or disable synchronizing your corporate email to your Galaxy Note II.

17. Scroll down to see more settings.

18. Touch to enable or disable synchronizing your corporate contacts to your Galaxy Note II.

19. Touch to enable or disable synchronizing your corporate calendar to your Galaxy Note II.

20. Touch to enable or disable synchronizing your corporate tasks to your Galaxy Note II.

21. Touch to enable or disable synchronizing SMS (text) messages you receive on your Galaxy Note II to your corporate Inbox.

22. Touch to enable or disable automatically downloading email attachments when your Galaxy Note II is connected to a Wi-Fi network.

23. Touch Next.

24. Touch Activate.

25. Enter a name for this email account. Use something meaningful that describes the purpose of the account, such as `Work Email`.

26. Touch Done to complete the setup.

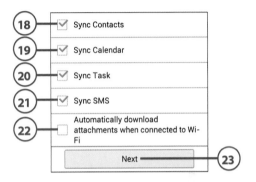

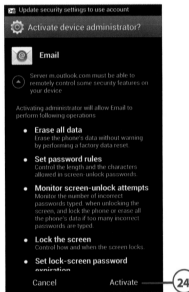

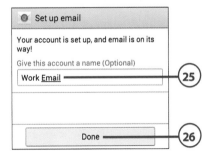

Removing an Account

To remove an account, from the Settings screen touch the type of account (for example, Microsoft Exchange ActiveSync) and then touch the account to be removed. Touch Remove Account.

CAN YOU TRULY KEEP WORK AND PRIVATE DATA SEPARATE?

More and more companies are adopting a Bring Your Own Device (BYOD) policy, which means that they expect you to use your personal phone to get access to company emails, contacts, calendar, and internal apps. As we have seen, your Galaxy Note II fully supports accessing your company's email system, but when you activate, you have to agree to allow your administrator control over your phone. This is not ideal as the administrator can see what apps you have installed, and he can send a self-destruct command to your Galaxy Note II, which means you lose all your private data and apps. Dual Persona is fast becoming the way for you to truly keep your private data private and not allow your company to wipe your phone or see what you have installed. A few companies today provide this service, including Enterproid (the product is called DIVIDE) and Good Technology (the product is called GOOD). The idea is that your Galaxy Note II has two personalities—a work persona and a private persona. All work data is kept in its own separate area on your phone, and your administrators have no control over the rest of your phone. Visit http://divide.com or http://good.com to learn more.

Add a New POP3 or IMAP Account

1. Pull down the Notification bar and touch the Settings icon.

2. Scroll down to Accounts and touch Add Account.

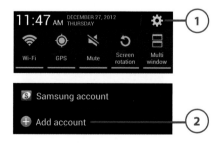

3. Touch Email.

4. Enter your email address.

5. Enter your password.

6. Touch Next.

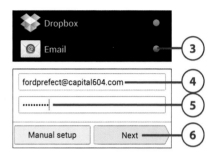

Why Manual Setup?

Your Galaxy Note II tries to figure out the settings to set up your email account. This works most of the time when you are using common email providers such as Yahoo! or Hotmail. It also works with large ISPs such as Comcast, Road Runner, Optimum Online, and so on. It might not work for smaller ISPs, in smaller countries, or if you have created your own website and set up your own email. In these cases, you need to set up your email manually.

7. Touch POP3 or IMAP. IMAP has more intelligence to it, so select that when possible.

8. Ensure that the information on this screen is accurate.

9. Touch Next.

Where Can I Find This Information?

If you need to manually set up your email account, you must have a few pieces of information. Always check your ISP's, or email service provider's, website, and look for instructions on how to set up your email on a computer or smartphone. This is normally under the Support section of the website.

Username and Password

On the Incoming Server and Outgoing Server screens, your username and password should already be filled out because you typed them in earlier. If not, enter them.

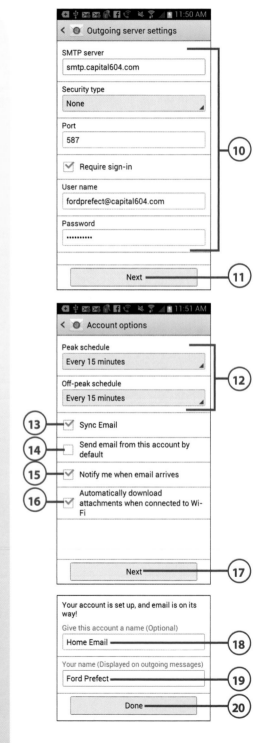

10. Ensure that the information on this screen is accurate.

11. Touch Next.

12. Touch to change the frequency in which email from this account synchronizes to your Galaxy Note II.

13. Touch to check the box if you want email to synchronize between this account and your Galaxy Note II.

14. Touch to check the box if you want email to be sent from this account by default.

15. Touch to check the box if you want to be notified when new email arrives into this account.

16. Touch to check the box if you want email to be automatically downloaded when you are connected to a Wi-Fi network.

17. Touch Next.

18. Enter a friendly name for this account, like **Home Email**.

19. Enter your full name or the name you want to be displayed when people receive emails sent from this account.

20. Touch Done to save the settings for this account and return to the Add Accounts screen.

Be Secure If You Can

If your mail provider supports email security, such as Secure Sockets Layer (SSL) or Transport Layer Security (TLS), you should strongly consider using it. If you don't, emails you send and receive go over the Internet in plain readable text. Using SSL or TLS encrypts the emails as they travel across the Internet so nobody can read them. Set this under the Advanced settings for the incoming and outgoing servers.

Working with the Email App

Now that you have added two new accounts, you can start using the Email application. Everything you do in the Email application is the same for every email account. The Email app enables you to either work with email accounts separately or in a combined view.

Navigate the Email Application

Before you learn how to compose or read emails, you should become familiar with the Email application.

1. Touch to launch the Email app.

2. Touch to switch between email accounts or select the Combined view, which shows all emails from all accounts.

3. Touch the star to mark an email as flagged.

4. Each color represents a specific email account.

5. Check boxes next to emails to select more than one. Then you can take actions against multiple emails at once, such as Mark as Unread, Delete, or Move to a New Folder.

6. Touch to compose a new email.

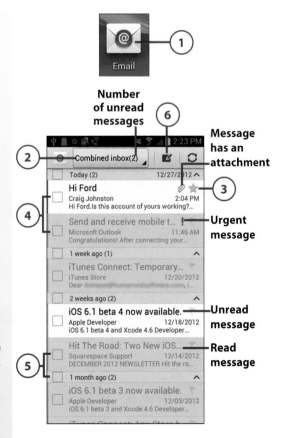

Number of unread messages 6

Message has an attachment

Urgent message

Unread message

Read message

Working in Batches

When you select multiple emails by checking the boxes next to them, you can take action on all the selected messages at once. You can mark the messages as unread, move them to a different folder, or delete them.

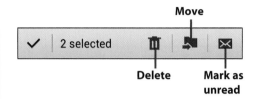

Move

Delete

Mark as unread

Landscape Mode

Because your Galaxy Note II has such a large screen, Samsung rewrote the Email app to support a Landscape mode. If you rotate your Galaxy Note II sideways, the Email app reconfigures to show the email list on the left and the actual email you are reading on the right.

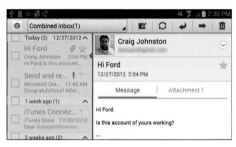

Email app in Landscape view

Compose an Email

1. Touch to compose a new email.

2. Enter one or more recipients. As you type, your Galaxy Note II tries to guess who you want to address the message to. If you see the correct name, touch it to select it. This includes names stored on your Galaxy Note II and in your company's corporate address book.

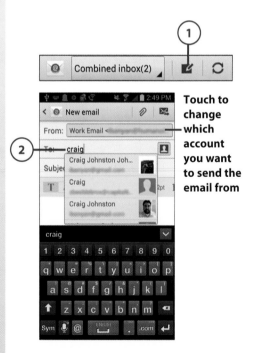

Touch to change which account you want to send the email from

3. Enter a subject.

4. Enter the body of the message. Use the formatting icons to change the font, font size, color, and other properties.

5. Touch to send the message.

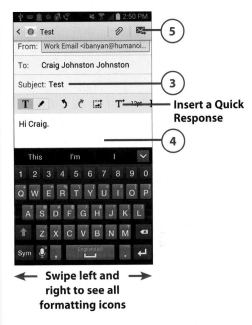

Insert a Quick Response

← Swipe left and → right to see all formatting icons

Can You Carbon Copy (Cc) and Blind Carbon Copy(Bcc)?

While you are composing your email, you can add recipients to the To field as described in step 2, but there are no Carbon Copy (Cc) and Blind Carbon Copy (Bcc) fields shown. However, you can add these fields by touching the Menu button and touching Add Cc/Bcc. After you do that, the Cc and Bcc fields display.

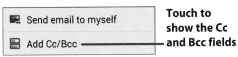

Touch to show the Cc and Bcc fields

Drawing in Your Email

Instead of just typing your email, you can draw in it. Pull out your S Pen and touch the Drawing Mode icon. Then draw in the area indicated. Touch the Pen Settings icon to change the style of instrument (brush, pen, and so on) and the color of the ink. Touch the Eraser icon and use the S Pen to erase parts of your drawing. Touch the Insert icon to insert images from the Gallery.

Drawing mode   Insert icon   Pen settings

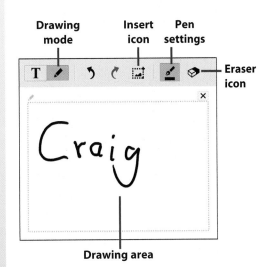

Eraser icon

Drawing area

Add Attachments to a Message

Before you send your message, you might want to add one or more attachments. You can attach any type of file, including pictures, video, audio, contacts, and location.

1. Touch the Attach icon.

2. Choose the type of attachment.

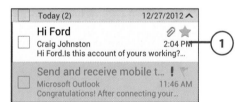

Scroll down to see all attachment types

Read Email

Reading messages in the Email application is the same regardless of which account the email has come to.

1. Touch an email to open it.

2. Touch to reply to the sender of the email. This does not reply to anyone in the Cc field.

3. Touch to forward the email.

4. Touch to expand the email header to see all recipients and all other email header information.

5. Touch to mark the message as flagged.

6. Touch to delete the message.

7. Touch to see the attachments.

8. Touch to play or view the attachment.

9. Touch to save the attachment to your phone.

10. Touch the Menu button to see more options.

11. Touch to mark the message as unread.

12. Touch to move the message to a different folder.

13. Touch to save the email as a file on your phone (outside the Email app).

14. Touch to print the email on a Samsung printer available on the Wi-Fi network.

15. Touch to compose a new email.

16. Touch to save the recipients of the email to your Contacts as a group.

17. Touch to change the font size used when reading the message.

18. Touch to add the sender to the Priority Sender list. Email from people in the Priority Sender list are displayed in the Priority Sender view.

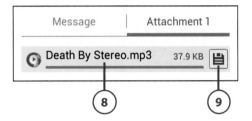

Change Email App Settings

1. Touch the Menu button.

2. Touch Settings.

3. Touch General Preferences.

4. Touch to change how auto-advance works. You can choose to either advance to a newer message, older message, or back to the message list.

5. Touch to change how many lines of the email are shown in the preview.

6. Touch to set the title of the email. You can set it as the email subject or the email sender.

7. Touch to enable or disable email deletion confirmation.

8. Touch to edit and add Quick Responses.

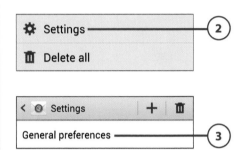

Quick Responses

Quick responses are words, phrases, sentences, or paragraphs of text that you create ahead of time and save as Quick Responses. While you are composing an email, you can choose to insert one or more of your Quick Responses. The idea is that it saves on typing the same things over and over.

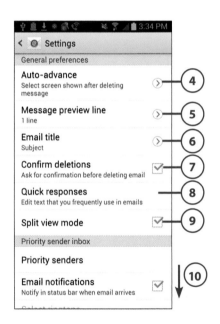

9. Touch to enable or disable Split View mode when you rotate your Galaxy Note II on its side.

10. Scroll down for more settings.

11. Touch to manage the Priority Sender list.

What Is the Priority Sender List?

Emails received from people who you have listed in the Priority Sender list are shown in the Priority Sender Inbox as well as in the regular Inbox. Opening the Priority Sender Inbox folder shows only emails from these people, which can be a way of filtering email so that you respond to the important people first and then switch to the regular Inbox and respond to everyone else.

12. Touch to enable or disable special email notifications when email is received into the Priority Inbox folder.

13. Touch to select the ringtone that plays when you are notified of new Priority Inbox emails.

14. Touch to also vibrate when being notified about new Priority Inbox emails.

15. Touch to go back to the main Settings screen.

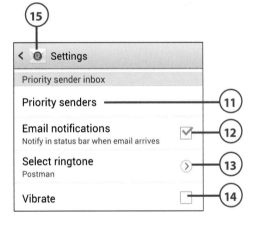

Corporate Account Settings

You are able to change your email signature as well as control what components are synchronized and how often they are synchronized. Repeat steps 1 and 2 from the "Change Email App Settings" task to get started.

1. Touch a corporate account.

2. Touch to change the account name.

3. Touch to add an email signature or edit the one you already have.

4. Touch to enable or disable using this account as the default account when composing email.

5. Touch to set whether you are Cc'd or Bcc'd on emails that you send.

6. Touch to enable or disable including any attachments on emails that you forward.

7. Touch to enable or disable showing images in emails.

8. Touch to enable or disable automatically downloading attachments when you are connected to Wi-Fi.

9. Scroll down for more settings.

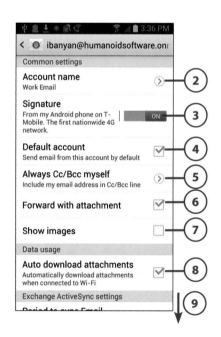

10. Touch to choose how many days of email to synchronize to your Galaxy Note II. You can choose between One Day and One Month, or choose All to synchronize every email ever received.

11. Touch to empty your Trash folder on the email server back in the office.

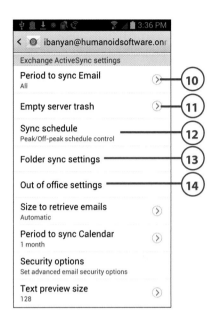

Why Empty the Office Trash Folder?

Step 11 describes how you can choose to empty your Trash folder back in the office. The reason that this is useful is sometimes your email administrator sets a limit on the size of your mailbox, and when you reach that limit, you are unable to send emails. By emptying your Trash folder back at the office, you might be able to clear a little bit of space in your mailbox so you can send that important email.

12. Touch to set the peak and off-peak schedule. By default, peak schedule is Monday to Friday 8:00 a.m. to 5:00 p.m. Off-peak is all other times. This setting enables you to change those times.

13. Touch to choose which folders you want to synchronize from your office email account and when they synchronize based on the peak and off-peak schedule.

14. Touch to set whether you are out of the office and your out-of-office message.

15. Touch to set the size of emails to retrieve, or leave it on Automatic to let the email administrator set this.

16. Touch to set how far back in the past your calendar syncs.

17. Scroll to set advanced security options, including whether you want to encrypt your emails, sign emails with an electronic signature, and email certificates to use with S/MIME (if your company supports it).

18. Touch to set the preview text size.

19. Scroll down for more settings.

20. Touch to change which device wins if there is a conflict between your phone and your email account back at the office.

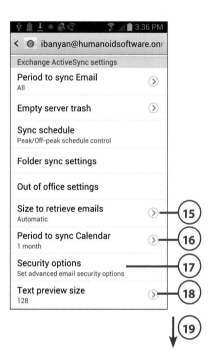

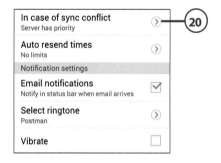

How Are There Conflicts?

A conflict can occur if you (or someone who has delegate access on your email account) makes a change in your mailbox using the desktop email client (like Outlook)—for example he moves an email to a folder—and you make a change on your Galaxy Note II—say you delete that same email. Now there is a conflict because an email has been both moved and deleted at the same time. If you set the server to have priority then the conflict is resolved using your rule that the server wins. In this example, the email is not deleted, but it is moved to a folder.

21. Touch to change the time range when your phone can resend emails that failed to send. No limits means it can resend anytime.

22. Touch to enable or disable being notified when new emails arrive for this account.

23. Touch to choose the ringtone that plays when you are notified of new email for this account.

24. Touch to enable or disable if the phone must also vibrate when the alert ringtone is played.

25. Scroll down for more options.

26. Touch to change the Exchange mail server settings for this account. This includes your account username and password if this has changed.

27. Choose what is synchronized to your phone.

28. Touch to return to the Settings main screen.

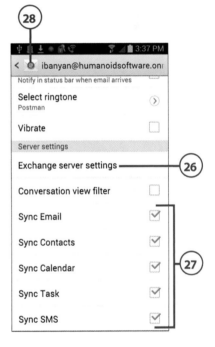

POP/IMAP Account Settings

1. Touch a POP or IMAP account.

2. Touch to change the account name.

3. Touch to change the name that recipients see when you send them email from this account.

4. Touch to add an email signature or edit the one you already have.

5. Touch to check the box if you want this account to be used as the default account when composing email.

6. Touch to set whether you want to be CC'd or Bcc'd on all emails that you send from this account.

7. Touch to enable or disable including any attachments in emails that you forward.

8. Touch to set how many recent messages are kept on your phone.

9. Touch to enable or disable showing images in emails to this account.

10. Scroll down for more settings.

11. Touch to set advanced security settings for this account, including choosing to encrypt emails, sign them with a digital signature, and manage encryption keys on your phone for use with encrypting emails.

12. Touch to enable or disable synchronizing email for this account.

13. Touch to enable or disable automatically downloading email attachments when your Galaxy Note II is connected to a Wi-Fi network.

14. Touch to change the size of emails retrieved from your email server.

15. Touch to change when your phone attempts to resend emails that have failed to send. You can choose a time range or set it to No Limits, which means anytime.

16. Touch to set the peak and off-peak time ranges. By default, peak schedule is Monday to Friday 8:00 a.m. to 5:00 p.m. Off-peak is all other times. This setting enables you to change those times.

17. Scroll down for more settings.

18. Touch to enable or disable being notified when email arrives for this account.

19. Touch to choose the ringtone that plays when you are notified of new email for this account.

20. Touch to enable or disable having vibration when the notification ringtone is played.

21. Touch to change the incoming server settings for this account.

22. Touch to change the outgoing server settings for this account.

23. Touch to return to the Settings main screen.

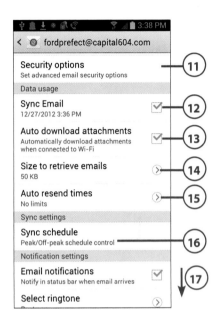
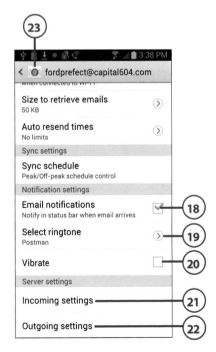

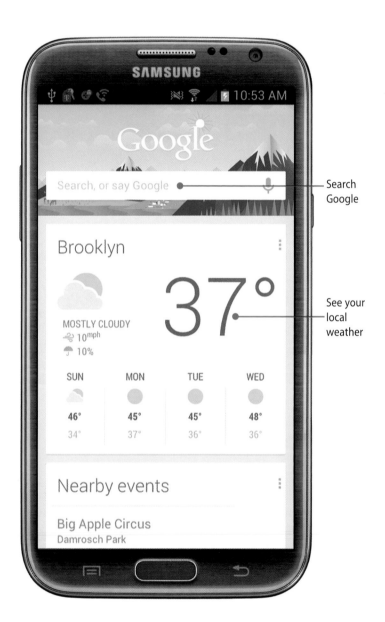

Search
Google

See your
local
weather

In this chapter, you find out how to use Google Maps, Navigation, and Google Now. Topics include the following:

→ Getting to know Google Now
→ Working with Google Maps
→ Using Google Maps with no data coverage
→ Getting around with Navigation

5

Google Now and Navigation

Your Galaxy Note II can be used as a GPS Navigation device while you are walking or driving around. The Galaxy Note II also includes a new app called Google Now that offers to provide you all the information you need when you need it.

Google Now

You can access Google Now from the Lock screen or from any screen and it enables you to search the Internet. The app also provides you information such as how long it will take to drive to work and game scores from your favorite teams.

Accessing Google Now

Before you even unlock your Galaxy Note II, you can access Google Now by sliding the Google icon up. You can also access Google Now from any app by touching and holding the Menu button.

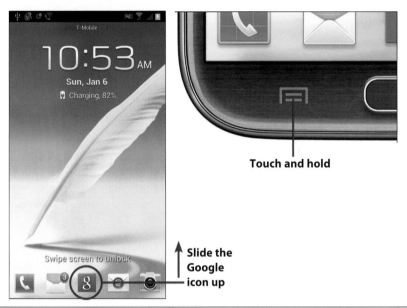

Touch and hold

Slide the Google icon up

Understand the Google Now Screen

1. Cards automatically appear based on your settings. Possibilities include teams you follow, upcoming meetings, weather where you work, and traffic on the way to work.

2. Touch and speak a request or search. You can also just say "Google" and then speak your request. Cards relevant to your search or request appear.

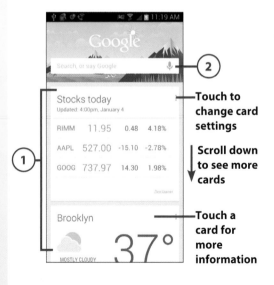

Touch to change card settings

Scroll down to see more cards

Touch a card for more information

Set Up Google Now

For Google Now to work for you, you should set it up correctly. This means setting up Google Now, but you also need to set up Google Maps, which is used heavily by Google Now.

1. Touch the Menu button.

2. Touch Settings.

3. Touch Google Now.

4. Touch to change how Google Now shows different cards. You can control if the card shows, what information it shows, and when it shows it.

5. Touch to save your changes and return to the main Settings screen.

6. Touch Voice.

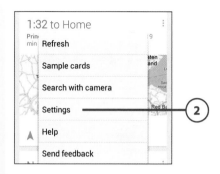

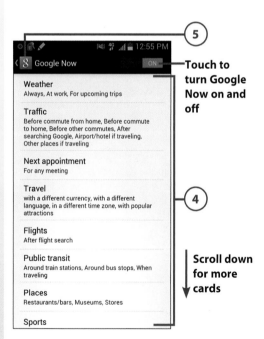

Touch to turn Google Now on and off

Scroll down for more cards

7. Touch to choose the language that Google Now uses.

8. Touch to set when you can speak to Google Now. The choices are Always or Only When You Are Using a Hands-free Device.

9. Touch to block or allow offensive words. Turning this on causes the Voice Search feature to hide any search results that contain offensive words.

10. Touch to enable or disable Hotword detection. When enabled, while Google Now is running, it is always listening for you to say "Google." When you do, a voice search launches.

11. Touch to download speech recognition software so you can do voice searches even when you're not connected to the Internet. You can download multiple languages.

12. Touch to enable or disable personalized voice recognition. When enabled, Google tries to better understand your accent to make for more accurate searches.

13. Touch to see your Google dashboard, which shows you all of your Google account information and enables you to manage settings for all of the Google services you use.

14. Touch to save your changes and return to the main Settings screen.

15. Touch to choose which apps installed on your Galaxy Note II are searched when you search using Google Now.

16. Touch to change which Google account you want to use for Google Now, and set whether you want to report your location information. (Disabling this severely limits the usefulness of Google Now.)

17. Touch to save your changes and return to Google Now.

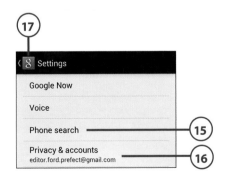

Set Up Google Maps

Because Google Now relies heavily on Google Maps, you need to change a few things in Google Maps and tell Google Maps where you live and work.

1. Touch to launch Google Maps.
2. Touch for Maps options.
3. Touch My Places.
4. Touch Starred.
5. Touch and hold to enter your home address, or edit it.
6. Touch and hold to enter your work address, or edit it.
7. Touch to close the My Places screen.
8. Touch the Menu button.
9. Touch Settings.
10. Touch Location Settings.
11. Make sure that Enable Location History is checked.
12. Touch the Back button to save your changes and return to the previous screen.

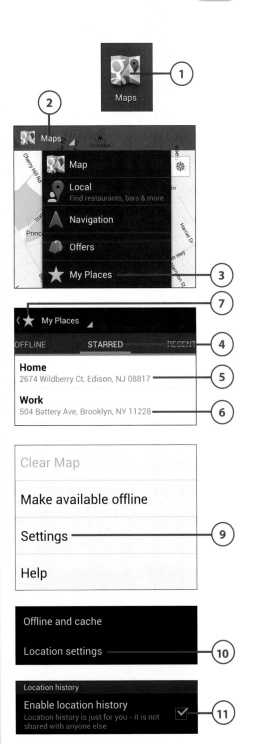

Google Maps

Google Maps enables you to see where you are on a map, find points of interest close to you, give you driving or walking directions, and provide extra layers of information, such as a Satellite view and traffic.

1. Touch to launch Google Maps.

2. Touch to type a search term.

3. Touch to get walking or driving directions from one location to another. You can also choose to use public transit or biking paths to get to your destination.

4. Touch to find local restaurants, coffee shops, bars, and attractions. This menu item also shows you special offers in the area.

5. Touch to add layers to the Map view. Layer options include restaurants, offers, traffic, a Satellite view, transit lines, biking paths, and Wikipedia entries for the area.

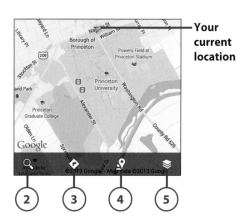

Your current location

Get Directions

Most people use Google Maps to get directions to where they want to go. Here is how.

1. Touch the Directions icon.

2. Touch to set the starting point or leave it as My Location (which is your current location).

3. Touch to choose a location from your Contacts, My Places, or a point on the map.

4. Type in the destination address.

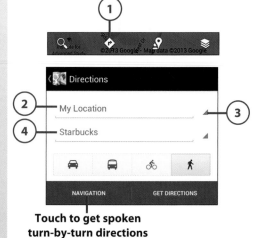

Touch to get spoken turn-by-turn directions

5. Touch to choose a location from your Contacts, My Places, or a point on the map.

6. Touch to use driving directions.

7. Touch to use public transportation.

8. Touch to use bike paths (if available).

9. Touch to walk to your destination.

10. Touch to see the directions on the map.

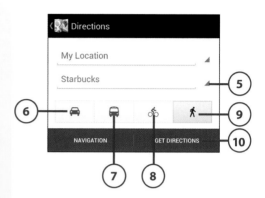

Public Transportation

If you choose to use public transportation to get to your destination, you have two extra options to use. You can choose the type of public transportation, including bus, subway, train, or tram/light rail. You can also choose the best route, including fewer transfers and less walking.

11. Touch to see the directions as a list.

12. Touch to launch the Navigation app to provide spoken turn-by-turn directions to your destination.

Adjust Google Maps Settings

1. Touch the Menu button.

2. Touch Settings.

3. Touch Display to tweak what is shown on the map. For example, you can change the bubble that appears above a landmark to show Navigation, Call, or Street View instead of the standard Get Directions.

4. Touch to remove all cached maps. This forces Google Maps to redownload new map areas as needed.

5. Touch to switch to another Google account to use Google Maps.

6. Touch to change your Google Map location setting.

7. Touch to change how Google Maps knows where you are. You can leave it as Detect Your Location (meaning Google Maps uses your GPS location information) or change it to a specific address.

8. Touch to enable or disable reporting your location from your Galaxy Note II. Combined with the next setting, you can update your location automatically so your friends can see where you are.

9. Touch to enable sharing your location with your friends. Which friends see your location is set in the next step.

10. Touch to manage which of your friends see where you are.

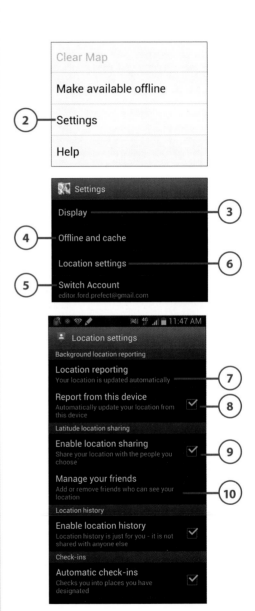

11. Touch to enable location history where Google Maps keeps track of where you have been. Having this enabled makes Google Now much better.

12. Touch to have Google Maps automatically check you into places you visit and have designated as places you visit a lot.

13. Scroll down for more settings.

14. Touch to enable check-in notifications, which enables Google Maps to suggest places for you to visit based on where you are.

15. Touch to manage your places, which includes places you check into often and places you want to mute (or do not want to hear about).

16. Touch the Back button to save your changes and return to the previous screen.

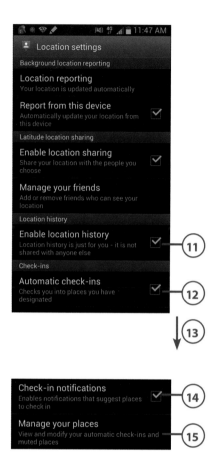

Use Offline Google Maps

Google Maps enables you to download small parts of the global map to your Galaxy Note II. This is useful if you are traveling and need an electronic map but cannot connect to a network to download it in real time.

1. Touch the Menu button.

2. Touch Make Available Offline.

3. Pinch to zoom out.

4. Move the blue selection square over the area you want to take offline. This area can be anywhere on the globe.

5. Touch Done to start downloading the map data to your Galaxy Note II.

How Much Map Can I Take Offline?

When selecting the area of the map to take offline, you are limited to about 100Mb of map data. However, you don't need to worry about the size of the data because if you have selected an area that is too large, Google Maps gives you a warning.

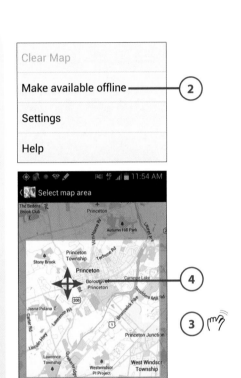

Your selection area is too large warning

It's Not All Good

Offline Maps Have Limited Use

If you download some map data to your Galaxy Note II, you can use it to zoom in and out of the area you downloaded and also see where you are on the map in real time while you have no network coverage. You cannot, however, get directions within the downloaded map area or use the Navigation app to get turn-by-turn directions. You also cannot search for things in the downloaded map area or see points of interest. So how useful is having map data already downloaded to your Galaxy Note II? It is useful to a point because it provides an electronic map while you're offline, but to be much more useful, you do need a network connection for directions and navigation. Because the map data is already downloaded, if you were to get a network connection and use that for driving directions, at least Google Maps would not need to download the map data in real time, which could save you a lot of money in data roaming charges.

Access Google Maps Offers

Google Maps has a feature that enables you to see offers from local businesses, shops, and restaurants. If there are coupons to use, you can use them right from your Galaxy Note II.

1. Touch and choose Offers.

2. Touch Offers Settings to make sure that you have this feature enabled. If you do already, skip to step 4.

3. Touch Notify Me of Nearby Offers.

4. Touch an offer to view it.

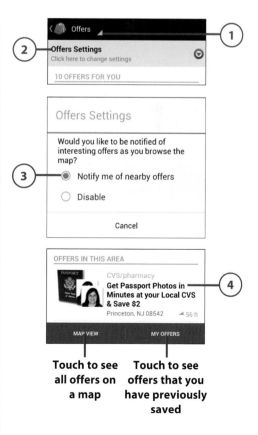

Touch to see all offers on a map   Touch to see offers that you have previously saved

5. Touch Use Now.

6. Touch Continue.

7. Follow the onscreen instructions. The offers can either be used via bar code, QR code, or Near Field Communications (NFC).

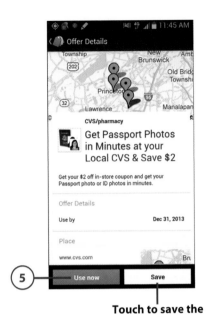

Touch to save the offer for later use

Locate Friends with Google Latitude

Google Maps includes Google Latitude that can show where your friends and family are on the map in real time.

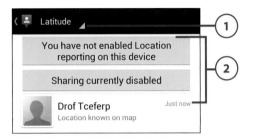

1. Touch and choose Latitude.

2. Touch to correct any settings that are required for Latitude to work.

3. Touch to see where all of your friends are plotted on the map.

4. Touch to request permission from your friends and family to allow you to see their location in Latitude.

5. Touch to check in to a location.

6. Touch to manually refresh the list of your friends. After your friends have given their permission, they are displayed here.

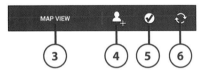

Navigation

The Navigation app provides the same functionality as built-in car navigation systems or portable navigation units you can buy and stick to your windshield. Combined with a good window mount, the Navigation app provides the same functionality but free of charge.

1. Touch to launch Navigation.

2. Touch to type a destination.

3. Touch to speak a destination. This allows you to speak the destination or name of destination instead of typing it.

4. Touch to see the map.

5. Touch to choose to go home. If you have not previously used this selection, you need to type in your home address.

6. Drive, cycle, or walk and listen to the audible turn-by-turn navigation instructions until you reach your destination.

7. Touch to show a list of actions.

8. Touch to adjust the route preferences and find alternative routes.

9. Touch to see the entire route in a list.

10. Touch to change the Navigation app setting for screen dimming, set a new destination, or search for a destination.

11. Touch to add or remove layers from the Navigation view. These include Satellite view, traffic, parking, gas stations, ATMs and banks, and restaurants.

12. Touch to turn off the voice prompts.

13. Touch to exit navigation.

Touch to choose between driving, cycling, or walking

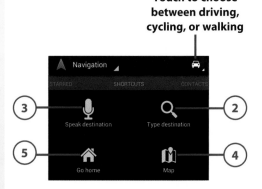

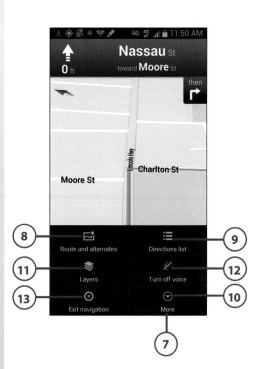

Clock in Bedside/
Dock mode

In this chapter, you find out how to set the time, use the Clock application, and use the Calendar application. Topics include the following:

→ Synchronizing to the correct time
→ Working with the Clock application
→ Setting alarms
→ Waking up with the latest weather, news, and your schedule
→ Working with the Calendar

Working with Date, Time, and Calendar

Your Galaxy Note II has a Clock application that you can use as a bedside alarm. The Calendar application synchronizes to your Google or Microsoft Exchange calendars and enables you to create meetings while on the road and to always know where your next meeting is.

Setting the Date and Time

Before you start working with the Clock and Calendar applications, you need to make sure that your Galaxy Note II has the correct date and time.

1. Touch the Settings icon.

2. Touch Date and Time.

3. Touch to enable or disable synchronizing time and date with the wireless carrier. It is best to leave this enabled as it automatically sets date and time based on where you are traveling.

Does Network Time Sync Always Work?

In some countries, on some carriers, time synchronization does not work. This means that when you get off the plane and turn Airplane mode off (see the Prologue, "Getting to Know Your Galaxy Note II," for information on Airplane mode), after a reasonable amount of time your time, date, and time zone will still be incorrect. In these instances, it is best to disable automatic date and time and manually set the time, date, and time zone yourself, and try it on automatic in the next country you visit or when you are back in your home country.

4. Touch to set the date if you choose to disable network synchronization.

5. Touch to set the time if you choose to disable network synchronization.

6. Touch to enable or disable synchronizing the time zone with the wireless carrier. It is best to leave this enabled as it automatically sets the time zone based on where you are traveling.

7. Touch to set the time zone manually if you choose to disable network synchronization.

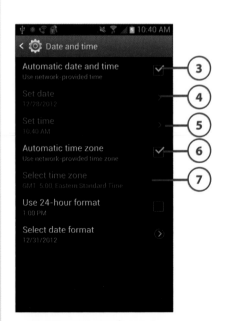

8. Touch to enable or disable the use of 24-hour time format. This format makes your Galaxy Note II represent time without a.m. or p.m. For example, 1:00 p.m. becomes 13:00 in 24-hour format.

9. Touch to change the way in which the date is represented. For example, people in the United States normally write the date with the month first (12/31/2010). You can make your Galaxy Note II display the date with the day first (31/12/2010) or with the year first (2010/12/31).

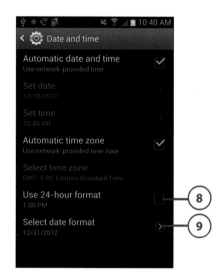

Clock Application

The Clock application is preinstalled on your Galaxy Note II and provides the functionality of a bedside clock and alarm clock.

Navigate the Clock Application

1. Touch the Clock icon.

2. Touch to create an alarm.

3. Touch to view and edit your alarms.

4. Touch to see the World Clock and manage the clocks on that screen.

5. Touch to use the Stopwatch.

6. Touch to use the Timer.

7. Swipe right to see the Desk Clock function.

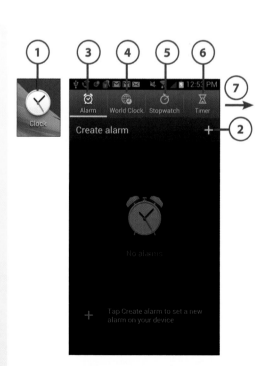

Manage Alarms

The Clock application enables you to set multiple alarms. These can be one-time alarms or recurring alarms. Even if you exit the Clock application, the alarms you set still trigger.

1. Touch to create a new alarm.

2. Use the up/down arrows to set the hours and minutes.

3. Touch to toggle between a.m. and p.m.

4. Touch the days of the week when you want the alarm to trigger. In this example, the alarm will sound on all days of the workweek but not on Saturday and Sunday.

5. Check this box if you want the alarm to repeat every week.

6. Touch to change the type of alarm. Your choices are Melody, Vibration, Vibration and Melody, and Briefing.

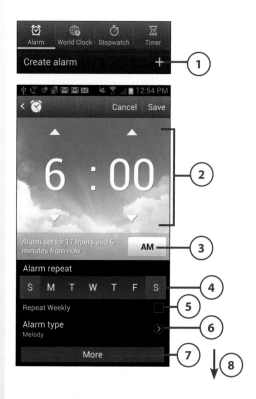

What Is Briefing?

If you choose the Briefing alarm type, you are awakened by the sound of the melody you chose to play, but your Galaxy Note II also reads you the weather, news of the day, and any appointments you have for that day.

---

7. Touch to see more alarm settings.

8. Scroll down to see the extra settings.

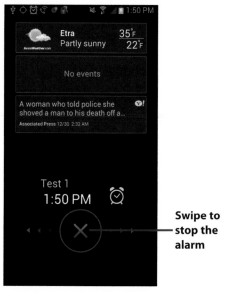

Swipe to stop the alarm

9. Slide to adjust the volume of the alarm.

10. Touch to change the alarm tone or melody that plays.

11. Touch to enable or disable Location Alarm. If you enable this, you are setting the alarm to only trigger when you are at the chosen location.

12. Touch to enable or disable the Snooze feature and set how long the snooze lasts.

13. Touch to enable or disable Smart Alarm. Smart Alarm plays a tune ahead of the alarm time to slowly start waking you up.

14. Touch to give the alarm a name.

15. Touch to save your new alarm.

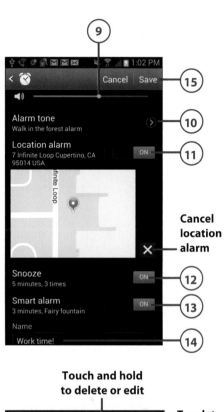

Editing or Deleting an Alarm

To edit or delete an alarm, touch and hold the alarm you want to edit or delete. When the pop-up window appears, make your choice. If you just want to quickly enable or disable an alarm, touch the Alarm Clock icon on the far right of an alarm.

Touch and hold to delete or edit

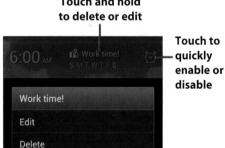

Touch to quickly enable or disable

Use the World Clock

The World Clock enables you to keep track of time in multiple cities around the world.

1. Touch to see the World Clock.

2. Touch to add a new city.

3. Type in a partial city name to find the city you want to add.

4. Touch a city to add it to the World Clock screen.

Managing Cities

To delete a city from your World Clock screen, or to rearrange the cities you've saved, touch the Menu button and choose Delete to select which cities to delete or Change Order to rearrange them.

Touch to see only cities in your country

Touch to see the globe and choose a city

Touch to choose cities to delete

Touch to rearrange the cities

Use the Desk Clock

You can manually select or automatically launch the desk clock when you insert your Galaxy Note II into a Samsung dock. This mode turns the Clock app into a desk clock or a bedside clock.

1. Swipe to the right.

2. Touch Desk Clock.

3. Touch to enable Dock mode. Read more about Dock mode in the next section.

4. Touch the Menu button to see the Settings menu item.

5. Touch to adjust the settings for the desk clock.

6. Touch to enable or disable displaying the calendar on the Desk Clock screen.

7. Touch to enable or disable displaying the weather on the Desk Clock screen.

8. Touch to choose Fahrenheit or Celsius and whether the weather is periodically updated.

9. Touch to adjust the settings for Dock mode. The next section covers the Dock mode settings.

10. Touch to save your changes and return to the Desk Clock screen.

Use Dock Mode

You can manually switch the desk clock into Dock mode, or Dock mode can be automatically activated when you insert your Galaxy Note II into a Samsung dock.

1. Touch to enable Dock mode (or insert your Galaxy Note II into a Samsung dock).

2. Touch to exit Dock mode and return to the desk clock.

3. Touch one of the shortcuts to launch the associated app.

4. After one minute, the screen dims, and just the date, time, and weather are displayed. The screen dims based on the light in the room.

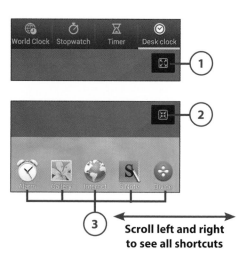

Scroll left and right to see all shortcuts

Touch anywhere to exit the dimmed screen

Change Dock Mode Shortcuts

You can add or remove shortcuts in Dock mode, which allows you to have quick access to the apps you need.

1. Touch the Menu button.

2. Touch Edit Shortcuts.

3. Touch to remove a shortcut.

4. Scroll to the right.

5. Touch to add a new shortcut.

6. Scroll down to see all available apps.

7. Touch to select an app to create a new shortcut.

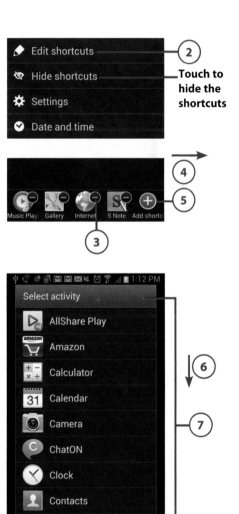

Touch to hide the shortcuts

Change Dock Settings

You can control how Dock mode works, and because the physical dock (if you have one) has ports for USB and audio, you can set how audio is output.

1. Touch the Menu button.

2. Touch Settings.

3. Touch to hide the status bar when in Dock mode.

4. Touch to choose the background. You can choose the default Dock wallpaper, choose an image from the Gallery app, or set it to use whatever you have chosen as the wallpaper for your Home screen.

5. Touch to enable or disable showing the Calendar in Dock view.

6. Touch to enable or disable showing the weather on the Dock screen.

7. Touch to choose Fahrenheit or Celsius and whether the weather is periodically updated.

8. Touch to set the brightness manually, or leave it set to automatic.

9. Touch to change settings relating to the physical dock.

10. Check the box to disable playing a sound when you insert your Galaxy Note II into the dock.

11. Touch to enable or disable using external speakers connected to the dock when docked and playing audio.

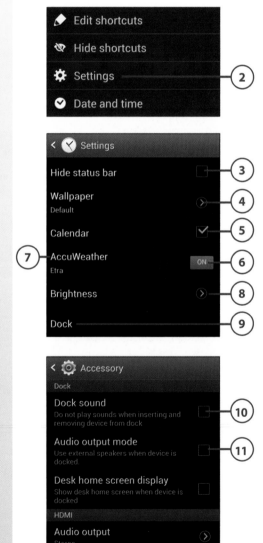

12. Touch to enable or disable automatically showing the Dock screen when you insert your Galaxy Note II into the dock. If unchecked, you just see the regular Home screen.

13. Touch to choose what kind of audio is output via the High-Definition Multimedia Interface (HDMI) cable when docked. You can choose Stereo or Surround.

14. Touch the Back button to save your settings and return to the Dock mode settings.

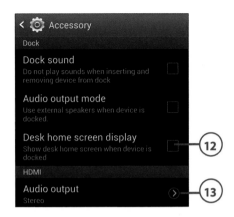

Using the Calendar Application

The Calendar application enables you to synchronize all of your Google Calendars under your primary Google account to your Galaxy Note II. You can accept appointments and create and modify appointments right on your phone. Any changes are automatically synchronized wirelessly back to your Google Calendar.

Navigate the Calendar Main Screen

The main screen of the Calendar app shows a one-day, one-week, or one-month view of your appointments. The Calendar app also shows events from multiple calendars at the same time.

1. Touch the Calendar icon.

2. Swipe left to go backward in time.

3. Swipe right to go forward in time.

4. Touch to show today's date.

5. Touch to have the Calendar view choices slide in from the right.

6. Choose a Calendar view.

7. Touch to switch to Writing mode, where you can draw over the calendar with the S Pen.

Drawing All Over Your Calendar

Instead of adding events to your calendar, you can just draw on the calendar as if it was a wall calendar or a page in a notebook. This feature only works when you are viewing the Month view and you are holding your Galaxy Note II in portrait orientation. When you switch into Writing mode as described in step 7, you can draw anything anywhere on the month. This is simply free-form drawing and is not translated into real events in your calendar; however, it's an easy and creative way to mark the calendar for yourself.

8. Touch to create a new event.

9. Touch to choose which calendars to display simultaneously.

Event Colors

The Calendar app can display one calendar or many calendars at the same time. If you choose to display multiple calendars, events from each calendar are color coded so you can tell which events are from which calendar.

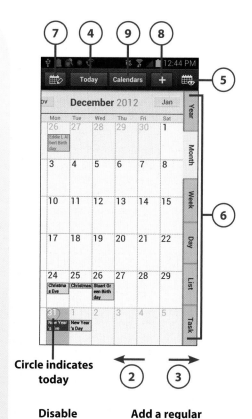

Circle indicates today

Disable Writing mode

Add a regular event

Switch between Writing and Touch modes

Choose Which Calendars and Task Lists to View

If you have set up multiple accounts, which might each have multiple calendars or task lists, you can choose which calendars the Calendar app shows at the same time. This task picks up from step 9 of the preceding task.

1. Check to display all calendars and task lists from all accounts.

2. Touch to expand an account to see all calendars and task lists it has.

3. Touch to enable or disable displaying the calendar or task list.

4. Touch to save your changes and return to the Calendar view.

Add a new account

Change Calendar Settings

1. Touch the Menu button.

2. Touch Settings.

3. Touch to switch the way that the calendar shows events when you touch to view them in the Month view. Your choice is to have a pop-up showing the Event view or a list of the events at the bottom of the screen.

4. Touch to switch the way that the calendar shows the Week view. Your choice is to have a Timeline view where the days are across the top and the hours of the day are below, or an Analog view where the days are all shown on the screen at once.

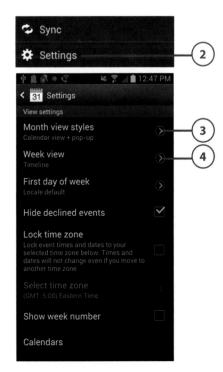

5. Touch to set the first day of your week. You can choose Saturday, Sunday, or Monday. You can also choose Locale Default, which means the locale determined by the time zone you are in controls what the first day of the week is.

6. Touch to enable or disable hiding events you have declined.

7. Touch to enable or disable using your home time zone when displaying the calendar and event times. When this is enabled, your home time zone is always used even when you are not traveling in it.

8. Touch to set your home time zone if you enabled Lock Time Zone in step 7.

9. Touch to enable or disable showing the week number. For example, March 26th is in week 13.

10. Scroll down for more settings.

11. Touch to change how the calendar is displayed when you switch to Writing mode.

12. Touch to enable or disable notifications for calendar events. You can also set whether you are alerted in the Notification bar only or with a pop-up alert.

13. Touch to choose the ringtone to play when you are being alerted for calendar events.

14. Touch to choose whether your Galaxy Note II should also vibrate when the event ringtone plays.

15. Touch to set the default event reminder time.

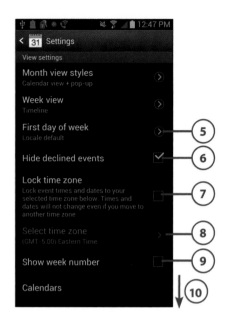

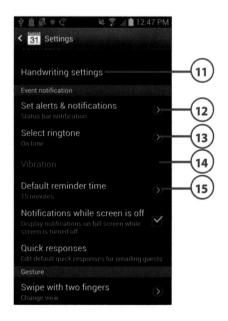

16. Touch to enable or disable being alerted even when your Galaxy Note II's screen is off.

17. Touch to edit the four built-in Quick Responses. Read more about Quick Reponses later in this chapter.

18. Touch to see an animation that shows how to use two fingers to change the Calendar view.

19. Touch to save your settings and return to the main Calendar screen.

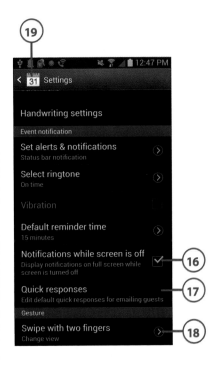

Add a New Event

While you're on the road, you can add a new appointment or event—and even invite people to it. Events you add synchronize to your Google and corporate calendars in real time.

1. Touch to add a new event.

A Quicker Way to Add an Event

You can quickly add a new event by touching and holding on the day on which you want to create the event and the time of day you want to create it.

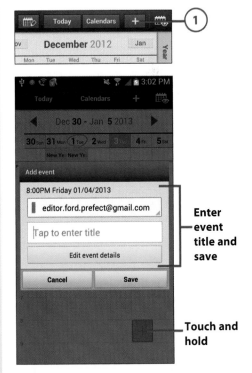

Enter event title and save

Touch and hold

2. Touch to select which calendar to add the event to.

3. Touch to enter a title for your event.

4. Touch to choose a sticker for your event. The stickers have images that help you visually categorize events.

5. Touch to select the start date and time of the event.

6. Touch to select the end date and time of the event.

7. Touch to select the time zone the meeting will be held in. This is useful if you will be traveling to the meeting in a different time zone.

8. Touch to mark the event as an all-day event.

9. Touch to set this as a recurring event. You can make it repeat daily, weekly, or monthly on the same date each month, but you can also set a meeting to repeat, for example, monthly but only every last Thursday regardless of the date.

10. Touch to add a new reminder.

11. Touch to remove a reminder.

12. Touch to change the type of reminder (Email or Notification) and how long before the event the reminder must trigger.

13. Scroll down to set more event settings.

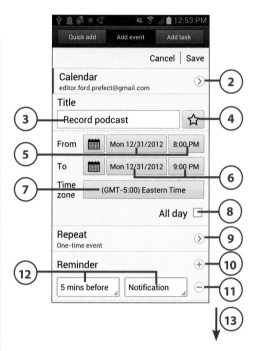

14. Enter where the event will take place. This can be a full physical address, which is useful because most smartphones can map the address.

15. Enter a description for the event.

16. Enter the event guests, or event invitees. As you type names, your Galaxy Note II retrieves matching names from your Contacts and your corporate directory. If the email addresses you are typing are compleyely unknown, type a semicolon between them to separate them.

17. Touch to remove a guest.

18. Scroll down to set more event settings.

19. Touch to choose how to show your availability during this event. You can choose Busy or Available.

20. Touch to choose the privacy of the event. You can choose Public or you can choose Private so only you can see it. If the event is being created on your corporate calendar, setting the event to Private means that people can see you are busy, but they cannot see the event details.

21. Touch to link an existing S Note to this event or write a new one.

22. Touch to link an image from the Gallery app to this event, or take a new picture.

23. Touch to save the event. Any attendees that you have added are automatically sent an event invitation.

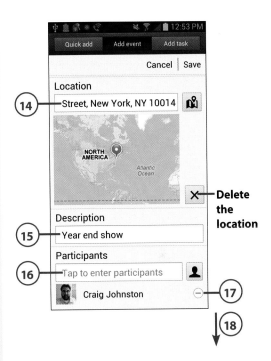

Delete the location

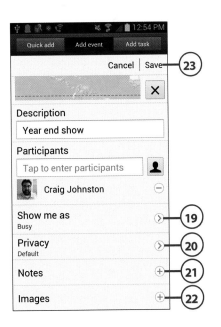

Editing and Deleting an Event

To edit or delete a calendar event, touch the event to see the event preview and then touch the event preview. After the event opens, touch the Menu button and choose either Edit or Delete. When you successfully delete an event, the Calendar application sends an event decline notice to the event organizer. So you don't have to first decline the meeting before deleting it because this is all taken care of automatically.

Respond to a Google Event Invitation

When you are invited to an event, you can choose your response right on your Galaxy Note II in the invitation email itself, or you can use the Calendar app.

Respond from the Email

The Google event invitation email allows you to respond in the email itself.

1. Touch to open the event invitation email.

2. Touch Yes, Maybe, or No to indicate whether you will attend.

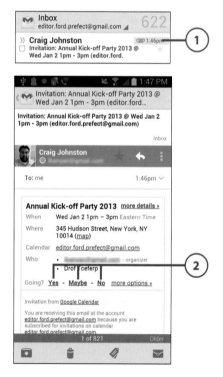

Respond from the Calendar

When you receive an invite, it is automatically inserted into your Google calendar but with no response selected.

1. Touch the new event.

2. Touch the event location to have it mapped in Google Maps or another mapping app that you have installed (such as Google Earth).

3. Touch to send your response.

4. Touch to save your changes.

Respond to a Corporate Event Invitation

When you are invited to an event, you can choose your response right on your Galaxy Note II in the invitation email itself, or you can use the Calendar app.

Respond from the Email

Your Galaxy Note II allows you to respond to an event invitation in the email itself.

1. Touch to open the event invitation email.

2. Touch to see the invitation responses.

3. Touch Accept, Tentative, or Decline to indicate whether you will attend. Alternatively, you can suggest a new event time.

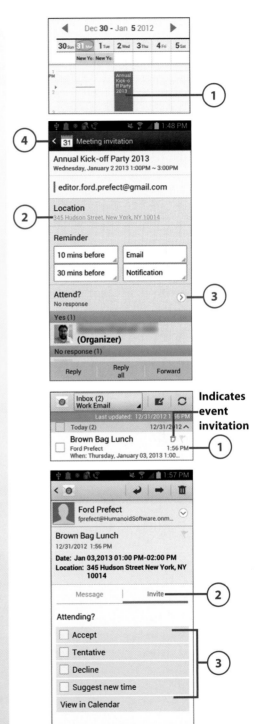

Respond from the Calendar

When you receive an invite, it is automatically inserted into your Google calendar with the Tentative response selected.

1. Touch the new event.

2. Touch the event location to have it mapped in Google Maps or another mapping app that you have installed (such as Google Earth).

3. Touch to choose your response or suggest a new time.

4. Choose Yes (Accept), Maybe (Tentative), or No (Decline). Alternatively, you can suggest a new time.

5. Choose whether you want to edit your response before sending it, send your response with no extra text, or do not send a response (your response is still recorded, just not sent).

Use Quick Responses

When you are notified of an upcoming event on your Galaxy Note II, you can choose to Snooze or Email Guests. When you choose to Email Guests, you can choose a Quick Response to send them.

1. Pull down the Notification bar and touch to email guests.

2. Choose one of your Quick Responses or write a custom message. Read more about editing your Quick Responses earlier in this chapter.

3. Choose which email app you want to use to send the Quick Response.

Touch to Snooze the reminder

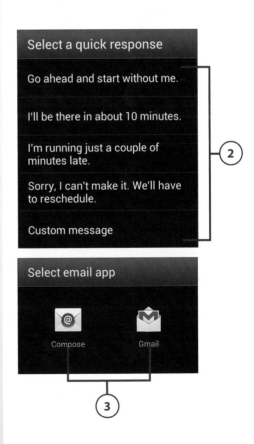

Add a Task

In addition to calendar events, you can add tasks to be completed.

1. Touch to add a new task.

2. Touch Add Task.

3. Touch to choose which account the task must be added to.

4. Enter a title for the task.

5. Choose when the task is due.

6. Touch to choose when you want to be reminded of the task.

7. Touch to choose the task's priority.

8. Enter a description for the task.

9. Scroll down to see more fields.

10. Touch to link an existing S Note to this task, or write a new one.

11. Touch to link an existing image to this task, or take a picture with the camera.

12. Touch to save the task.

Marking a Task as Completed

To mark a task as completed, switch to Task view. Check the box to the left of the task to mark it as completed.

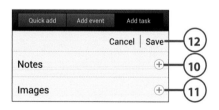

Check the box to mark the task as complete

Add, search, and manage your contacts

In this chapter, you become familiar with your Galaxy Note II's contact-management application, which is called Contacts. You find out how to add contacts, synchronize contacts, join duplicate contacts together, and even how to add a contact to your Home screen. Topics include the following:

→ Importing contacts
→ Adding contacts
→ Synchronizing contacts
→ Creating favorite contacts

Contacts

On any smartphone, the application for managing contacts is essential because it is where you keep all of your contacts' information. On the Galaxy Note II, this application is called simply Contacts. It is the central hub for many activities, such as calling and sending text messages (SMS), multimedia messages (MMS), or email. You can also synchronize your contacts from many online sites, such as Facebook and Gmail, so as your friends change their Facebook profile pictures, their pictures on your Galaxy Note II change as well.

Adding Accounts

Before you look around the Contacts app, add some accounts to synchronize contacts from. You already added your Google account when you set up your Galaxy Note II in the Prologue, "Getting to Know Your Galaxy Note II."

Adding Facebook, Twitter, LinkedIn, and Other Accounts

To add accounts for your online services such as Facebook, Twitter, LinkedIn, and so on to your Galaxy Note II, install the apps for those services from Google Play. Please see how to install apps in Chapter 11, "Working with Android Apps." After they are installed and you have signed in to them, if you visit the Accounts settings as shown in the following sections, you see new accounts for each online service.

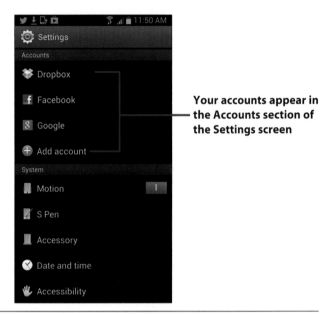

Your accounts appear in the Accounts section of the Settings screen

1. From the Home screen, pull down the Notification bar.

2. Touch the Settings icon.

3. Scroll up or down as necessary to reach the Accounts section, and then touch Add Account.

4. Touch Microsoft Exchange ActiveSync.

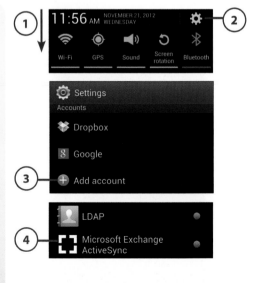

5. Type the email address for the account.

6. Touch Password and type the password.

7. Touch Show Password if you want to see the password rather than the dots the Galaxy Note II shows for security. Seeing the password can be helpful when entering complex passwords.

8. Touch Next.

Providing ActiveSync Server Information

Your Galaxy Note II tries to work out some information about your company's ActiveSync setup. If it can't, it prompts you to enter the ActiveSync server name manually. If you don't know what it is, you can try guessing it. If, for example, your email address is dsimons@allhitradio.com, the ActiveSync server is most probably webmail.allhitradio.com. If this doesn't work, ask your email administrator.

9. Touch OK to agree that your mail administrator may impose security restrictions on your Galaxy Note II after you connect to the Exchange server.

Remote Security Administration

Remote Security Administration is another way of saying that when you activate your Galaxy Note II against your work email servers, your email administrator can add restrictions to your phone. These can include forcing a device password, imposing the need for a very strong password, and requiring how many letters and numbers the password must be. It also means that your email administrator has the power to remotely wipe your Galaxy Note II so that it is put back to factory defaults. This is normally done if you lose your phone or it is stolen.

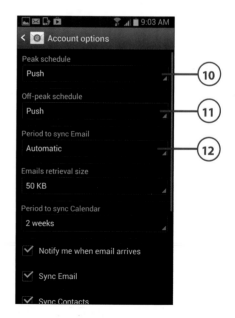

10. Touch to choose how often your Galaxy Note II receives Exchange email during peak hours.

Push and Other Options for Getting Email

Push means that as email arrives in your Inbox at work, it is delivered to your phone. You can set it to Manual, which means that your Galaxy Note II checks for email only when you open the Email app. You can also set the checking interval from every 5 minutes to every hour.

11. Touch to choose how often your Galaxy Note II receives Exchange email during off-peak hours.

12. Touch to choose how many days in the past email is synchronized to your Galaxy Note II or set it to All to synchronize all email in your Inbox.

13. Touch to choose the largest email size to retrieve. You can choose from 5KB to 100KB, choose All to retrieve all messages no matter how big they are, or choose Automatic to use the server's settings.

14. Touch to choose how long a period of calendar appointments to synchronize. Your choices are 2 weeks, 1 month, 3 months, 6 months, or All calendar.

15. Check this box to receive a notification when email messages arrive.

16. Check this box to sync your email messages with the server. Normally, you will want to do this.

17. Scroll down the screen and then check this box to enable synchronizing your corporate contacts to your Galaxy Note II.

18. Check this box to enable synchronizing your corporate calendar to your Galaxy Note II.

19. Check this box to enable synchronizing your corporate task list to your Galaxy Note II.

20. Check this box to enable synchronizing your SMS messages to your Galaxy Note II.

21. Check this box to make your Galaxy Note II automatically download email attachments when connected to a Wi-Fi network.

22. Touch Next.

What to Synchronize

You might decide that you don't want to synchronize all your work information to your Galaxy Note II. You might decide to just synchronize email, and not the calendar, or maybe just the calendar but not the contacts and email. Unchecking these boxes enables you to choose the information you don't want to synchronize.

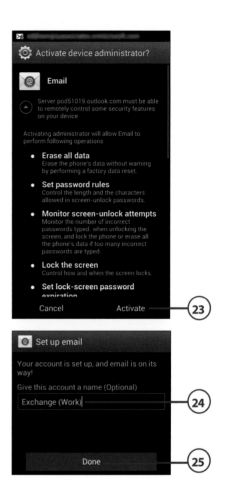

23. Touch Activate.

24. Enter a name for this email account. Use something meaningful that describes the purpose of the account such as `Exchange (Work)`.

25. Touch Done to complete the setup.

Removing an Account

To remove an account, open the Settings screen and touch the account to be removed. On the screen for the account, touch the account in the Accounts list and then touch Remove Account on the screen that appears.

Navigating Contacts

The Contacts app consists of four screens: Phone, Groups, Favorites, and Contacts. Normally, the Contacts app displays the Contacts screen first, showing your list of contacts, but you can navigate to any of the other screens by touching its tab.

1. From the Home screen, touch the Contacts icon.

2. Touch to add a new contact.

3. Touch to switch to the Phone app. From the resulting screen, you can dial a number on the keypad.

4. Touch to see your contact groups. See more information about creating contact groups in the later section titled "Create Contact Groups."

5. Touch to see your list of favorite contacts.

6. Touch to see all contacts.

7. Touch to search for a contact.

8. Touch a contact to see all information about her.

9. Touch a contact picture (or picture placeholder) to see the Quick Connect bar.

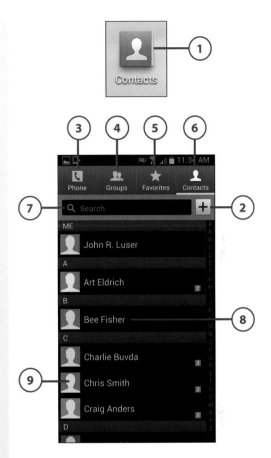

Quick Connect Bar

When you touch a contact picture, the Quick Connect bar displays. This bar enables you to quickly access different ways of communicating with the contact. If the icon list extends off the screen, swipe left to reveal further icons.

Phone call   Email   Address

Internet call   Video call

Check a Contact's Status

If you have added contacts that belong to social networks such as Facebook, you can check their statuses right from the Contacts app.

1. Touch a contact.

2. Touch to view the contact's Facebook profile.

Edit a Contact

When you need to, you can easily change a contact's existing information or add further information to it.

1. Touch the contact you want to edit.

2. Touch to open the contact record for editing.

3. Touch to enter a name prefix, middle name, or name suffix.

4. Touch a – sign next to an existing field to delete it.

5. Touch to change the field subcategory. For example, you can change a phone number's subcategory from Mobile to Home.

6. Touch + to add a new field in a specific category. In this example, touching + enables you to add a new phone number and choose its subcategory, such as Work.

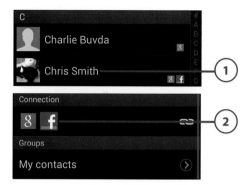

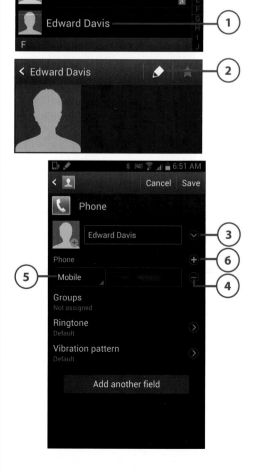

7. Touch to put the contact in a contact group. The Galaxy Note II comes with built-in groups, including ICE Emergency Contacts, Co-Workers, Family, and Friends, but you can also create as many other groups as you need.

8. Touch to assign a different ringtone to calls from the contact. By giving important contacts distinctive ringtones, you can easily identify important calls.

9. Touch to assign a different vibration pattern to calls from the contact. Vibration patterns help you identify important calls when you have silenced the ringer.

10. Touch to add a new field to the contact record. Extra fields include things such as the contact's phonetic name (to help you pronounce it correctly), IM (Instant Messaging) addresses, Notes, and Relationship, which you use to specify how someone is related to the contact—for example, an assistant or manager.

11. Touch Save to save the changes to the contact record.

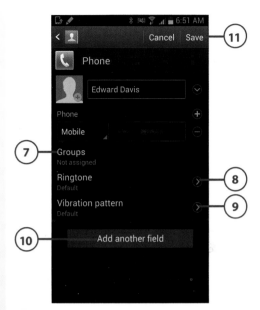

Add a Contact Photo

A contact record on your Galaxy Note II includes a contact photo when you link a social network account to the contact or when you import a contact record that includes a photo (for example, from a vCard file). You can manually add a picture as needed, either from an existing file or by taking a photo.

1. Touch the contact.

2. Touch the contact photo to open the Contact Photo dialog.

3. Touch to add a photo already saved on your Galaxy Note II.

4. Touch the album that contains the photo.

5. Touch the photo you want to use.

6. Drag the cropping box to select the area of the photo you want to use for the contact photo.

7. Drag the outside of the cropping box to expand or contract it as needed.

8. Touch Done to save the cropped photo as the contact photo.

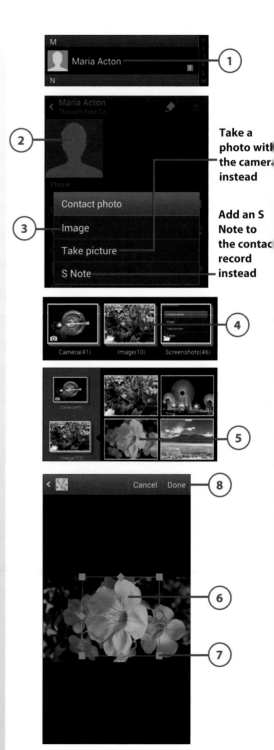

Take a photo with the camera instead

Add an S Note to the contact record instead

Adding and Managing Contacts

As you add contacts to your work email account or Google account, those contacts are synchronized to your Galaxy Note II automatically. When you reply to or forward emails on your Galaxy Note II to an email address that is not in your Contacts, those email addresses are automatically added to the contact list or merged into an existing contact with the same name. You can also add contacts to your Galaxy Note II directly.

Add a Contact from an Email

To manually add a contact from an email, first open the email client (either Email or Gmail) and then open a message. Please see Chapter 4, "Email," for more on how to work with email.

1. Touch the blank contact picture to the left of the sender's name.

2. Touch Create Contact.

3. In the Save Contact To dialog, touch the account to which you want to save the contact.

4. Type the contact's name.

5. Touch Save to save the contact.

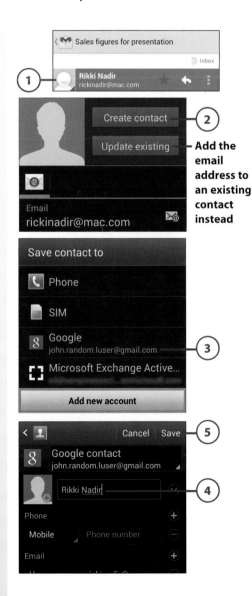

Add the email address to an existing contact instead

Add a Contact Manually

1. Touch the Contacts icon on the Home screen.

2. Touch to add a new contact.

3. Touch to select which account you add the new contact to. For example, you might want to add the new contact to your work email account instead of to your personal account.

4. Type the person's full name, including any middle name. Your Galaxy Note II automatically populates the first name, middle name, and last name fields.

5. Touch to choose a contact picture.

6. Touch and drag up to scroll down to reach other fields.

7. Touch Save to save the new contact.

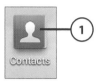

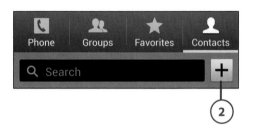

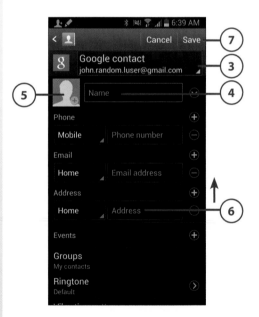

Add a Contact from a vCard

A vCard is a file that contains a virtual business card—which can include a contact's name, job title, email address, physical address, phone numbers, and so on. You can easily exchange vCards with other people by attaching them to email messages or instant messages. When you receive a vCard, you can import it into the Contacts app as a new contact by using the following steps.

1. Touch View under the attachment that has the .vcf extension.

Choosing the App for vCard Files

If your Galaxy Note II displays the Complete Action Using dialog when you touch View to open a vCard file, touch Contacts and then touch Always.

2. Touch to select the account to add the new contact to. For example, you might want to add the new contact to your work email account instead of to your personal account.

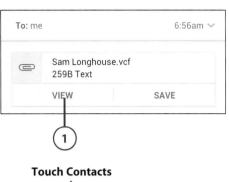

Touch Contacts

Touch Always

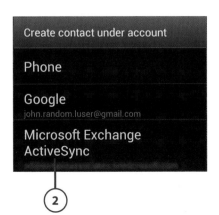

Add a Contact Using Near Field Communications

Your Galaxy Note II has Near Field Communications (NFC) functionality built in. This enables you to exchange contact cards between NFC-enabled smartphones or to purchase items in a store by holding your Galaxy Note II near the NFC reader at the checkout counter. If you encounter someone who has an NFC-enabled smartphone, or she has an NFC tag that contains her business card, follow these steps to import that information.

1. Hold the other person's smartphone back to back with your Galaxy Note II and give the command for sharing via NFC, or hold the NFC tag close to the back cover of your Galaxy Note II. Your Galaxy Note II's screen dims and the phone plays a tone to indicate that it is reading the NFC information.

2. Touch to select which account you want to add the new contact to. For example, you might want to add the new contact to your work email account instead of to your personal account.

Create contact under account

Phone

Google
john.random.luser@gmail.com

Microsoft Exchange
ActiveSync

Manage Contacts Settings

To make the Contacts app display contacts the way you prefer, you can customize it. For example, you can choose the contact list display order and whether to display contacts using their first names first or last names first.

1. Touch the Contacts icon on the Home screen.

2. Touch the Menu button.

3. Touch Settings.

4. Touch to choose the sort order of the list of contacts in the Contacts app. You can sort the list by first name or last name.

5. Touch to choose how each contact is displayed. You can display contacts with the first name first or the last name first.

6. Touch Settings to save the settings and return to the Contacts app.

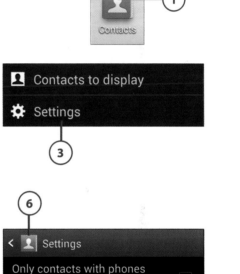

Create Contact Groups

You can create contact groups—such as Friends, Family, Inner Circle—and then divide your contacts among them. This can be useful if you don't want to search through all your contacts. For example, to find a family member, you can simply touch the Family group and see only family members.

1. Touch the Groups icon from the Contacts main screen.

2. Touch the Menu button.

3. Touch Create.

4. Enter a name for your new group.

5. Optionally, touch to set a specific ringtone for the group. You can use the ringtone and vibration pattern (discussed next) to make calls from the group easy to distinguish.

6. Optionally, touch to set a specific vibration pattern for the group.

7. Touch to add members to the group.

8. Touch the check boxes next to contacts' names to select each member of the group.

9. Touch Done.

10. Touch Save to save the group.

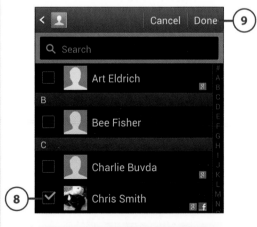

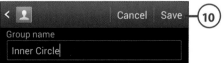

Change the Contacts in a Contacts Group

1. Touch the Groups icon on the Contacts main screen.

2. Touch the group to edit.

3. Touch to add a contact to the group.

4. Touch the Menu button.

5. Touch Remove Member.

6. Touch the contact or contacts you want to remove.

7. Touch Done to remove the contact and save the changes.

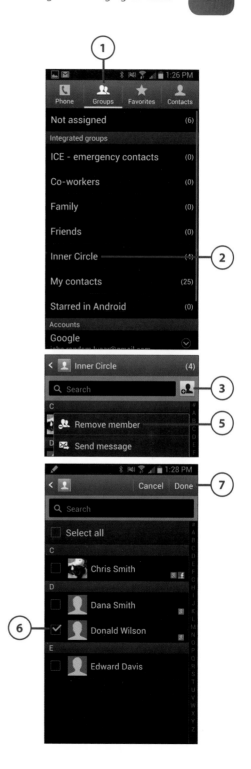

Choose Which Contacts to Display

You can choose to hide certain contact groups from the main contacts display. For example, you can choose to show only contacts from Twitter. You can also choose which contact groups in each account to include.

1. Touch the Contacts icon on the Home screen.

2. Touch the Menu button.

3. Touch Contacts to Display.

4. Touch to display all contacts from all accounts.

5. Touch an account to show only contacts in that account.

6. Touch to choose a customized selection.

7. Touch to customize which groups in each account are displayed.

8. Touch to expand an account to see subgroups of contacts.

9. Touch to select or deselect a subgroup of contacts.

10. Touch Done to save your settings.

Join and Separate Contacts

As you add contacts to your Galaxy Note II, they are automatically merged if the new contact name matches a name that's already stored. Sometimes you need to manually join contacts together or separate them if your Galaxy Note II has joined them in error.

Join Contacts Manually

1. Touch the contact that you want to join a contact to.

2. Touch the Menu button.

3. Touch Join Contact.

4. Touch the contact you want to join with.

5. Touch the contact's name to return to the Contacts screen.

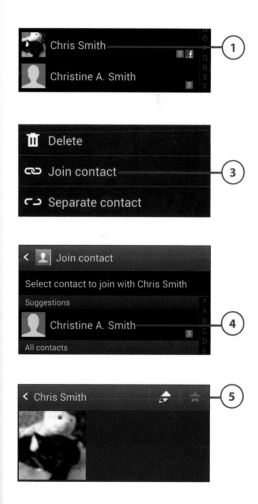

Separate Contacts

1. Touch the contact that you want to separate.

2. Touch the Menu button.

3. Touch Separate Contact.

4. Touch the contact you want to separate.

5. Touch OK to separate the contacts.

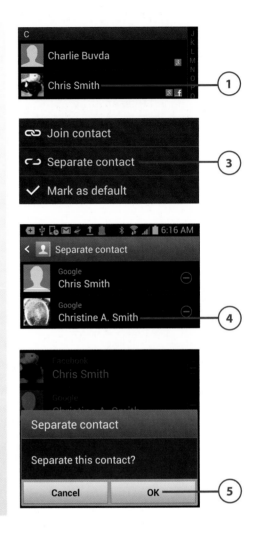

Adding a Contact to Your Home Screen

If you communicate with some contacts so much that you are constantly opening and closing the Contacts application, you can save time and effort by adding a shortcut to the contacts on the Home screen.

1. Touch the Launcher icon.

2. Touch Widgets.

3. Swipe right until you see the Contact widget.

4. Touch and hold the Contact widget.

5. While still holding the widget, position the widget on the Home screen and release your finger. The list of contacts appears automatically.

6. Touch the contact you want to add to the Home screen.

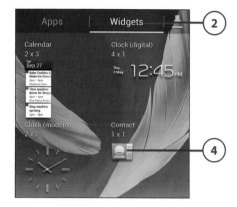

>>>Go Further

IMPORTING AND EXPORTING CONTACTS

You can import any contacts that are stored on your SIM or vCards that you have saved to your Galaxy Note II's internal storage. You can also export your entire contact list to your Galaxy Note II's SIM card or to a USB storage device. To access the import/export functions, touch the Menu button and touch Import/Export.

Touch to import or export contacts

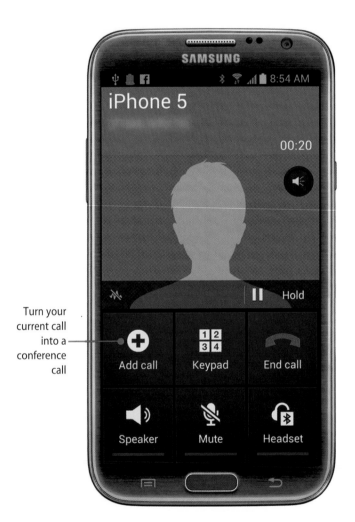

Turn your current call into a conference call

In this chapter, you find out how to make and take phone calls and send instant messages on your Galaxy Note II. Topics include the following:

→ Making phone calls
→ Making conference calls
→ Sending and receiving text messages
→ Sending and receiving multimedia messages

8

Phone, SMS, and MMS

As a cellular phone, your Galaxy Note II includes powerful features that enable you to make phone calls swiftly and easily. Your Galaxy Note II can also send both text-only instant messages and multimedia instant messages by using the Messaging app.

Phone

With the Phone app, you can quickly make and receive calls across the cellular network. When you need to talk to more than one other person, you can easily turn your current call into a conference call.

Open and Navigate the Phone App

The Phone app contains four tabs that enable you to make calls in various ways and to track the calls you receive.

1. On the Home screen, touch Phone.

Opening the Phone App from the Lock Screen

If your Galaxy Note II uses swipe to unlock the Lock screen, you can open the Phone app directly from the Lock screen. Instead of swiping open space, touch the Phone icon on the Lock screen and swipe from there.

2. If the Keypad tab does not appear at the front, touch Keypad.

3. Touch the keys to dial a number.

4. If the Phone app displays a suggested contact with a matching number, you can tap the contact if it is the one you want.

5. Touch to place the call.

6. Touch Logs to see a list of the calls and messages you have placed and sent.

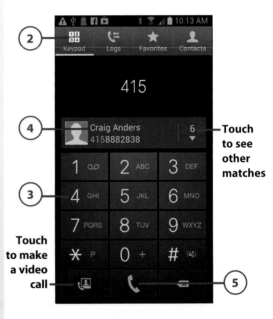

Touch to see other matches

Touch to make a video call

Making Your Logs Display the Information You Need

At first, the Phone app displays all your logs, but you can narrow down the view to specific logs so you can more easily find the calls and messages you need. You learn to do this later in this chapter.

7. Touch Favorites to see lists of Favorites and Frequently Contacted contacts.

8. Touch Contacts to display your full contacts list in the Contacts app.

9. Touch Phone to return to the Phone app.

Receive a Call

When someone phones your Galaxy Note II, you can accept the call, reject it, or reject it and send a text message.

Accept a Call

1. When the phone rings, look at the contact name if it is available or the phone number if it is not, and decide whether to take the call.

2. Touch and drag to accept the call.

3. Touch to switch to the speaker.

4. Touch to enable extra volume on the speaker.

5. Touch to switch to the headset.

6. Touch to mute the call. Touch again to turn off muting.

7. Touch to place the call on hold. Touch Unhold, which replaces the Hold button, when you are ready to restart the call.

8. Touch to end the call.

Reject a Call

If you do not want to accept the call, you can reject it so that it goes to your voicemail.

1. When the phone rings, touch and drag to reject the call.

The call goes to voicemail, and your Galaxy Note II displays the screen you were using before the call came in.

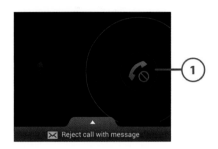

Reject a Call and Send a Message

Instead of simply declining a call and sending it to your voicemail, you can send a text message straight back to the caller. Your Galaxy Note II provides a selection of canned messages for general needs. You can also create your own messages or type custom messages for particular calls.

1. When the phone rings, touch and drag up to open the Reject Call with Message shade.
2. Touch to send one of the canned messages.
3. Touch to create and send a custom message.
4. Type the message.
5. Touch to send the message.

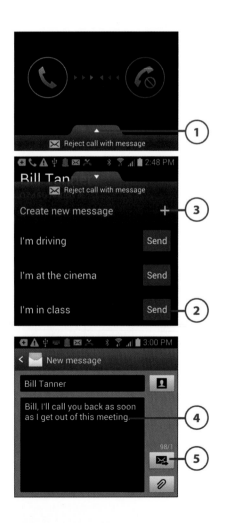

Creating Your Own Canned Reject Messages

To create and save your own canned reject messages, open the Phone app and touch the Menu button. On the menu, touch Call Settings. On the Call Settings screen, touch Set Reject Messages. On the Reject Messages screen, touch Create to create a new message, or touch an existing message to open it for editing.

Handle Missed Calls

If you miss a phone call, you can quickly locate it in the Phone app's logs so that you can return it.

Shows the number of missed calls

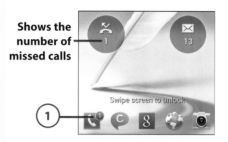

1. Swipe to unlock your Galaxy Note II and go straight to the Phone app. When there are missed calls, the Phone app displays the Logs tab first.

2. If the Logs tab is not displayed, touch to display it.

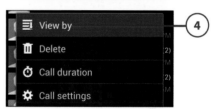

3. If you want to change the logs displayed, touch the Menu button.

4. Touch View By.

5. Touch the button you want to filter by. For example, touch Missed Calls.

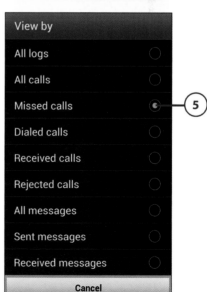

6. Touch a call to see its details.

7. Touch to phone the contact back.

Place a Call

When you need to make a phone call, you can dial it manually using the keypad. But usually you can make a call more quickly by placing the call from a contact entry or by using your voice.

Dial with the Keypad

You can use the keypad to dial a call both when you need to call a number for which you do not have a contact and when you can remember part of the number for a contact.

1. In the Phone app, touch the Keypad tab to bring it to the front.

2. Start typing the phone number. If you are typing to recall a number, type the part you remember.

3. If Phone suggests the correct number, touch to dial it.

4. Alternatively, touch to display other matching numbers.

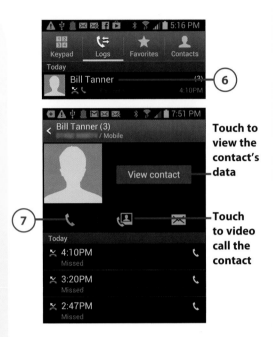

Touch to view the contact's data

Touch to video call the contact

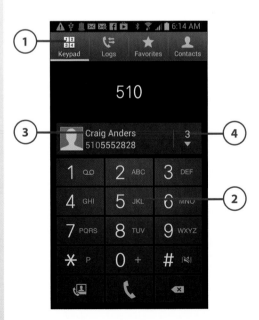

5. Touch the number you want to dial. If none of the suggestions are correct, touch Cancel and finish dialing the number manually.

6. Touch to dial the number.

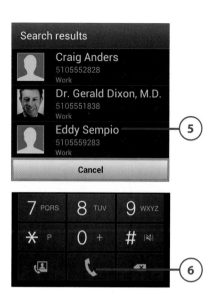

Dial from a Contact Entry

If you know you have a contact entry for the person you want to dial, you can start from that contact entry.

1. In the Phone app, touch the Contacts tab to bring it to the front. Android switches from the Phone app to the Contacts app.

2. Touch the contact to display the contact's details.

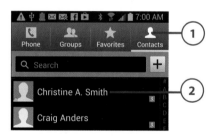

Starting a Call from the Contacts App

Instead of launching the Phone app and then touching the Contacts tab to go to the Contacts app, you can start a call directly from the Contacts app. Touch Contacts on the Home screen or the Apps screen to launch the Contacts app, touch the contact to display his or her details, and then touch the Call button or the Video Call button.

3. Touch the number you want to call.

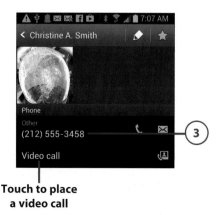

Touch to place a video call

Dial Using Your Voice

Your Galaxy Note II also enables you to dial calls using your voice.

1. On the Apps screen, touch S Voice.

2. Say, "Call," followed by the contact's name; if the contact has multiple phone numbers, say the type of number as well. For example, say, "Call Dana Smith mobile," or, "Call Maria Ramirez work."

3. Wait while S Voice dials the call. The Dialing screen appears.

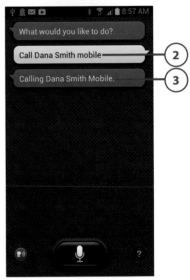

Control a Call and Make Conference Calls

After accepting or establishing a phone call, you can control it from the Call screen.

1. Touch Hold to put the call on hold. When you do this, the person at the other end of the call normally receives an automatic announcement that you have put them on hold.

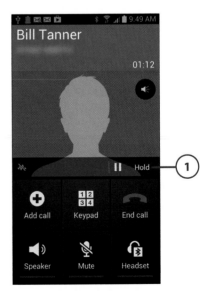

2. Touch Unhold to remove the hold.

3. Touch Keypad to display the keypad.

4. Touch the keys to navigate through voicemail systems.

5. Touch Hide when you no longer need the keypad.

6. Touch Mute to mute the call. Touch again to remove muting.

7. Touch Headset to switch the audio to the headset.

8. Touch Speaker to switch the audio to the speaker.

9. Touch to enable or disable extra volume.

10. Touch to end the call.

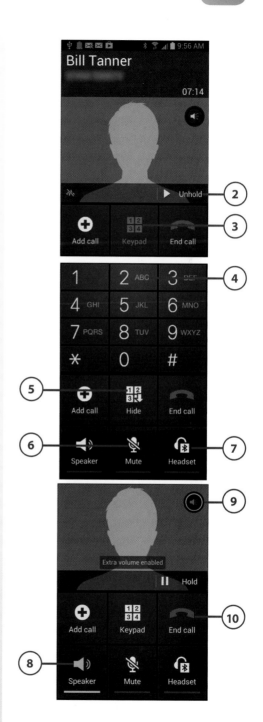

Using Other Apps During a Call

During a call, you can use most other apps freely, but you cannot play music or video. You can take photos with the Camera app, but you cannot shoot videos. To switch to another app, either use the Recent Apps list or press the Home button and use the Apps screen as usual. While you are using another app, your Galaxy Note II displays a green bar at the top of the screen to remind you that you are in a call. When you return to the Phone app, your Galaxy Note II displays a panel of options. Touch Return to Call in Progress to go back to your call.

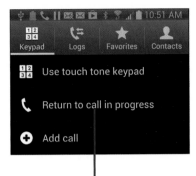

Touch to return to your call

Make Conference Calls

You can quickly turn your current call into a conference call by adding further participants.

1. On the call screen, touch Add Call.

2. Dial the call in the most convenient way. For example, touch the Contacts tab, touch the contact in the list, and then touch the Call button on the contact's details screen.

3. When your Galaxy Note II has established the new call, the original caller is on hold. Touch Merge to merge the calls.

4. When you are ready to finish the call, touch End Call.

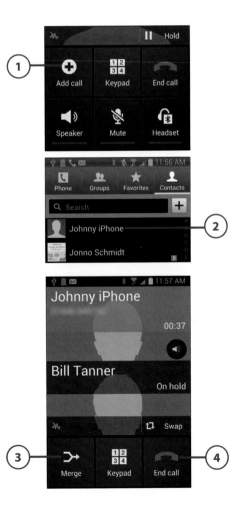

Configure the Phone App

To make the Phone app work your way, you can configure its settings.

1. On the Home screen, touch Phone.

2. Touch the Menu button.

3. Touch Call Settings.

4. Touch to set up Auto Reject mode.

5. Touch to edit your canned reject messages.

What Does Auto Reject Mode Do?

Your Galaxy Note II's Auto Reject mode can automatically reject either all calls or only the numbers on a list you provide. Automatically rejecting all calls can be useful for meetings and social occasions when you do not want to be disturbed. Automatically rejecting specific numbers enables you to avoid calls from people you do not want to talk to. You can turn Auto Reject mode on and off by moving the Auto Reject Mode switch.

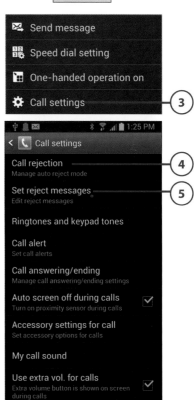

Choose between rejecting all numbers and specific numbers

Set up your list of numbers to reject

Turn Auto Reject mode on and off

6. Touch to choose your ringtones, keypad tones, and vibrations for calls.

7. Touch to choose options for vibrations, cell status tones, and alerts during calls. You can choose whether your Galaxy Note II vibrates when someone answers your call and when they hang up. You can also choose which status tones and alerts to receive during calls and which to suppress.

8. Touch to choose whether pressing the Home key answers an incoming call and whether pressing the Power button ends an ongoing call.

9. Touch to turn off the Galaxy Note II's proximity sensor during calls.

10. Touch to choose Phone settings for wired headsets and Bluetooth headsets.

11. Choose to customize how the audio on phone calls sounds. You can choose among Soft Sound, Clear Sound, Optimized for Left Ear, and Optimized for Right Ear options, or choose Off to use standard audio.

12. Touch to make the Extra Volume button appear during calls so you can pump up the sound if it is too quiet.

13. Scroll down and touch to make the Galaxy Note II ring more loudly when it detects it is in a pocket or a bag.

14. Touch to set up call forwarding for voice calls and video calls.

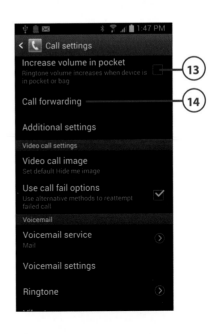

15. Touch to choose further settings, including Caller ID, Call Waiting, and Noise Reduction.

16. Touch to set a default image that appears in video calls when you hide yourself.

17. Touch to allow your Galaxy Note II to use alternative technologies to establish video calls that it cannot make directly.

18. Touch to set up your voicemail service.

19. Touch to adjust voicemail settings.

20. Touch to choose your ringtone for announcing voicemail.

21. Scroll down.

22. Touch to choose vibration settings for voicemail.

23. Touch to manage your accounts for making calls across the Internet.

24. Choose when to use Internet calling: for all calls, even when a mobile network is available; for Internet calls only; or to prompt you for each call.

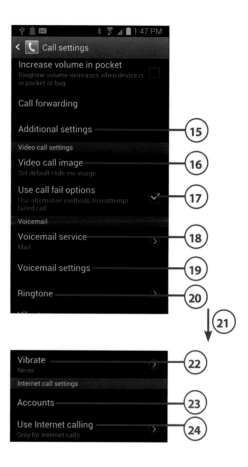

SMS and MMS

Short Message Service (SMS), also known as text messaging, has been around for a long time and is still used today as the primary form of communication for many younger phone users. Multimedia Message Service (MMS) is a newer form of instant messaging that can contain pictures, audio, and video as well as text. Your Galaxy Note II can send and receive both SMS and MMS messages.

Get to Know the Messaging App

The Messaging app is what you use to send and receive text messages. This app has all the features you need to compose, send, receive, and manage these messages.

1. Touch the Messaging icon on the Home screen.

2. Touch to compose a new text message.

3. Touch the sender's picture to show the Quick Connect bar.

4. Touch a message thread to open it.

5. Touch the Menu button to change the Messaging app settings or to delete message threads.

6. Look here for how many unread messages are in a message thread.

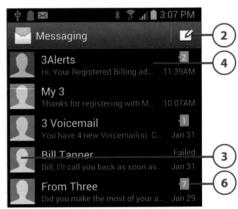

Manage Settings for the Messaging App

You use the settings of the Messaging app to manage how the app handles your SMS and MMS messages. Before you actually start working with SMS and MMS, let's take a look at the settings.

1. Touch the Menu button.

2. Touch Settings.

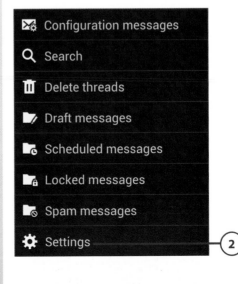

3. Touch to choose which colors and styles of bubbles the app uses for messages.

4. Touch to choose which background the app uses for messages.

5. Touch to use a split view when you turn your Galaxy Note II to landscape orientation.

6. Touch to enable changing text size by pressing the volume buttons.

7. Touch to enable or disable automatically deleting old messages when the limits you set in steps 8 and 9 are reached.

8. Touch to change the text message limit per thread (or conversation). The maximum number you can enter is 999. When the limit is reached, Messaging deletes messages within the thread or conversation using the first in, first out (FIFO) method.

9. Touch to change the multimedia message limit per thread (or conversation). The maximum number you can type is 999. When the limit is reached, messages within the thread or conversation are deleted using the first in, first out (FIFO) method.

10. Touch to edit your list of text templates. These are canned messages such as, "When can we meet?" and, "Please call me when you get this message."

11. Scroll down for more settings.

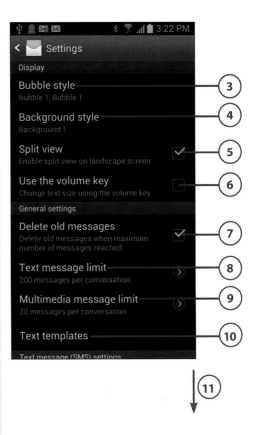

12. Touch to enable or disable delivery reports. Although your Galaxy Note II supports this feature, it is not well supported by other phones, so you might not get delivery reports from some recipients.

13. Touch to manage the text messages stored on your Galaxy Note II's SIM card.

What Does the Manage SIM Card Messages Command Do?

Many old cell phones store text messages on the SIM card and not in the phone's memory. If you have just upgraded from an older phone, you might still have text messages on the SIM card that you would like to retrieve. Touch Manage SIM Card Messages on the Settings screen in the Messaging app to display the Manage SIM Card Messages screen. You can then copy the messages to your Galaxy Note II's memory and copy the senders to your contacts in the Contacts app.

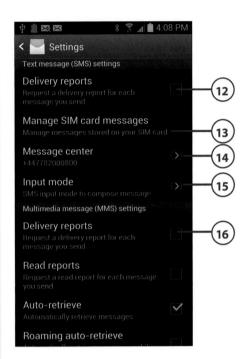

14. Touch to change your message center number. This is the number at your carrier that the Galaxy Note II contacts to retrieve your messages.

15. Touch to choose the input method for composing SMS messages. Your choices are GSM alphabet, Unicode, or Automatic. Change the default setting only if you are sure you need to.

16. Touch to enable or disable automatically requesting a delivery report for each multimedia message you send.

17. Touch to enable or disable a read report for each multimedia message you send.

What's the Difference Between a Delivery Report and a Read Report?

A delivery report indicates that the message has reached the destination device. A read report indicates that the message has been opened for viewing. There is still no guarantee that whoever opened the message has actually read it, let alone understood it.

18. Touch to enable or disable automatically retrieving multimedia messages.

19. Touch to enable or disable automatically retrieving multimedia messages when roaming.

Don't Auto-Retrieve MMS While Roaming

Disable the automatic retrieval of multimedia messages when you travel to other countries because automatically retrieving these messages when you're roaming can result in a big bill from your provider. International carriers love to charge large amounts of money for people traveling to their countries and using their networks. The only time it is a good idea to leave this enabled is if your carrier offers an international SMS or MMS bundle where you pay a flat rate up front before leaving. When you have auto-retrieve disabled, you see a Download button next to a multimedia message. You have to touch it to manually download the message.

20. Scroll down for more settings.

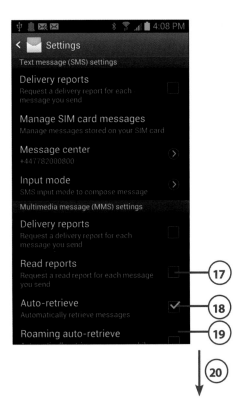

21. Touch to choose the Creation mode, which controls which content you can include in multimedia messages.

What Is the Creation Mode for Multimedia Messages?

The Creation mode feature lets you control which content Messaging allows you to include in messages. Choose Restricted to have the Galaxy Note II prevent you from including content that the recipient might not be able to receive or view. Choose Warning to have the Galaxy Note II warn you about such content but allow you to proceed. Choose Free to be able to include potentially problematic content without warning.

22. Touch to enable or disable a warning when you add content to an SMS message that makes it change to an MMS message.

23. Touch to enable or disable receiving messages "pushed" from the server. Push messages arrive at your Galaxy Note II shortly after they arrive at the server, which is usually faster than waiting until the Galaxy Note II checks for messages.

24. Touch to choose how to handle remote requests to load services. Your choices are Always, Prompt, and Never.

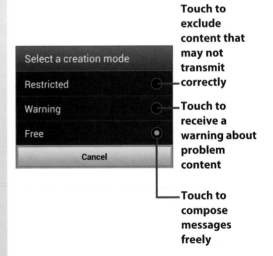

Touch to exclude content that may not transmit correctly

Touch to receive a warning about problem content

Touch to compose messages freely

It's Not All Good

What Setting Should I Choose for Service Loading?

Samsung's Service Loading feature has been used for attacks that remotely wipe smartphones without the owner's consent. Because of this danger, never choose Always as the Service Loading setting. Choose Prompt if you want your Galaxy Note II to let you decide about service loading requests. Choose Never if you prefer to suppress service loading requests.

Touch to be prompted before loading services

25. Touch to enable or disable receiving Citizens' Band (CB) messages.

26. If you enable receiving CB messages, touch to configure the channels on which you receive them.

27. Touch to enable or disable receiving notifications when messages arrive.

28. Touch to select the ringtone that announces incoming messages.

29. Scroll down for more settings.

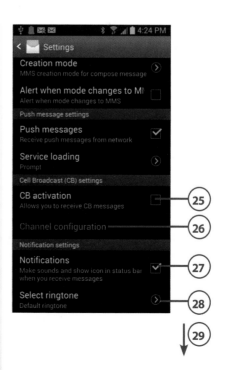

30. Touch to enable or disable vibration for message notifications.

31. Touch to choose how often your Galaxy Note II repeats a message alert. Your choices are Once, Every 2 Minutes, or Every 10 Minutes.

32. Touch to enable or disable the display of a preview of each incoming message in the status bar.

33. Touch to enable or disable adding a signature to each message you send. A signature is predefined text—for example, a sign-off salutation and your name.

34. If you enable adding a signature, touch this button and then enter the text of the signature.

35. Touch to enable or disable the settings for detecting spam messages. Spam messages are unwanted commercial messages.

36. If you enable spam settings, touch to register a phone number as a sender of spam. Your Galaxy Note II then blocks this number.

37. If you enable spam settings, touch to build a list of phrases that identify messages as being spam.

38. Scroll down to reach the final setting.

39. Touch to enable or disable blocking of all senders who are not in your contacts.

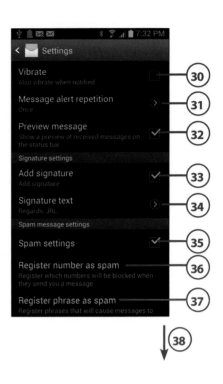

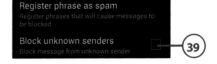

Compose Messages

When you compose a new message, you do not need to make a conscious decision whether it is an SMS message or an MMS message. As soon as you add a subject line or attach a file to your message, your Galaxy Note II automatically treats the message as an MMS message.

Here is how to compose and send messages.

1. Touch to compose a new message.

2. Start typing the recipient's phone number, or if the person is in your contacts, type the name. If Android finds a match, touch the mobile number.

3. Touch and start typing your message.

4. Touch to send your message.

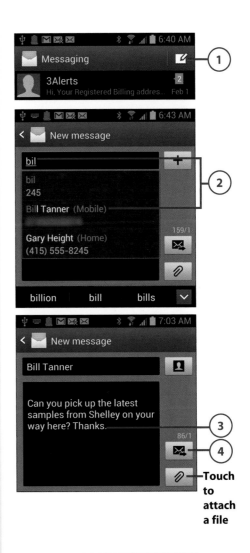

Inserting Smiley Icons

To insert smiley icons (or emoticons), touch the Menu button and then touch Insert Smiley. In the Insert Smiley dialog, scroll down if needed, and then touch the smiley you want to insert.

Touch to attach a file

Touch the smiley you want to insert

MESSAGE LIMITS AND MESSAGES

>>>Go Further

Text messages can only be 160 characters long. To get around this limit, most modern phones simply break up text messages you type into 160-character chunks. Your Galaxy Note II displays a readout showing the number of characters remaining and the number of messages it will send: The readout starts at 160/1 when you begin a new message and runs down to 1/1, then starts at 145/2 (because there is some overhead on linking the messages). The phone receiving the message simply combines them all together into one message. This is important to know if your wireless plan has a text message limit. When you create one text message, your Galaxy Note II might actually break the message into two or more.

31/2 —— **Message count indicator**

Attach Files to Messages

If you want to send a picture, audio file, or video along with your text message, all you need to do is attach the file. Attaching a file turns your SMS message into an MMS message.

1. Touch to attach a file.

2. Touch to attach a picture already stored in your Gallery app.

3. Touch to take a picture and attach it.

4. Touch to attach a video already stored in your Gallery app.

5. Touch to capture a video and attach it.

6. Touch to attach an audio file that is already stored on your Galaxy Note II.

7. Touch to record audio and attach it.

8. Touch to attach an S Note document.

9. Touch to attach an S Planner item.

10. Touch to attach your location.

11. Touch to attach a contact record from the Contacts app.

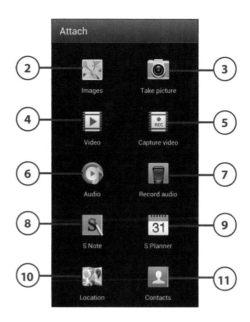

It's Not All Good

Is It Worth Attaching Files?

Attaching files to text messages is not as useful as you might desire. Most carriers limit the attachment size to around 300KB. This means that you can only really attach about 60 seconds of very low-quality video; pictures with low resolution, high compression, or both; and very short audio files. The Messaging app automatically compresses larger picture files to make them small enough to send, but you will often find that it simply refuses to send video files because they are too large. Choosing the option of capturing pictures, capturing video, or recording audio when you choose to attach is the only way you can guarantee that the files are small enough. This is because when you do this, the camera and audio recorder apps are set to a mode that makes them take low-quality pictures and record low-quality audio.

Receive Messages

When you receive a new SMS or MMS message, you can read it, view its attachments, and even save those attachments to your Galaxy Note II.

1. When a new SMS or MMS message arrives, your Galaxy Note II plays a ringtone and displays a notification in the status bar.

2. Pull down the notification shade to see newly arrived messages.

3. Touch a message alert to display the Messaging app.

4. Touch to display the message.

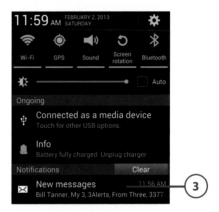

5. Touch an attachment to open it for viewing.

6. Touch and hold a message to display the Message Options dialog. Skip to step 8 for more about the additional options.

7. Touch to write a reply to the message.

8. Touch to delete the message. This deletes just the message and not the entire thread.

9. Touch to copy the message text so you can paste it elsewhere.

10. Touch to lock the message against deletion.

11. Touch to save the attachment to your Galaxy Note II.

12. Touch to forward the message and attachment to someone else.

13. Touch to view the message details, such as its size and the date and time it was sent.

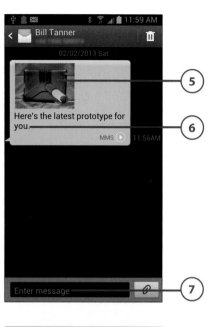

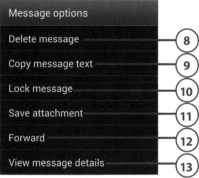

Usable Content

If a text message contains links to websites, phone numbers, or email addresses, touching those links makes the Galaxy Note II take the appropriate action. For example, when you touch a phone number, your Galaxy Note II calls the number; when you touch a web link, the Galaxy Note II opens the page in Chrome or your other default browser.

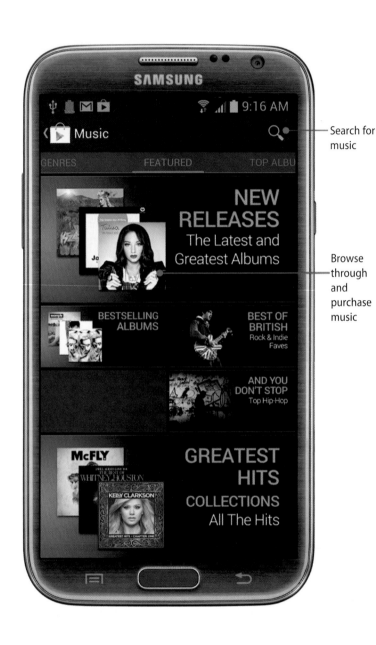

Search for music

Browse through and purchase music

In this chapter, you discover your Galaxy Note II's audio and video capabilities, including how your Galaxy Note II plays video and music, and how you can synchronize audio and video from your desktop or laptop computer or Google Music. This chapter also covers how to take pictures and videos. Topics include the following:

→ Using Google Music for music
→ Using the Gallery app for pictures and video
→ Applying video effects
→ Enjoying videos with the YouTube app

Audio, Video, Photos, and Movies

Your Galaxy Note II is a powerful multimedia smartphone with the ability to play back many different audio and video formats. The large screen enables you to turn your Galaxy Note II sideways to enjoy a video in its original 16:9 ratio. You can also use your Galaxy Note II to search YouTube, watch videos, and even upload videos to YouTube right from your phone. Android version 4 fully embraces the cloud, which enables you to store your music collection on Google's servers so you can access it anywhere.

Enjoying Music with the Music Application

To get the most out of music on your Galaxy Note II, you probably want to use the Play Music app, which enables you to listen to music stored on your phone as well as from your collection in the Google Music cloud. If your Galaxy Note II does not include the Play Music app, you need to install it first.

Install the Play Music App

Before installing the Play Music app, touch Apps on the Home screen and look through the list of apps. If Play Music is already installed, skip ahead to the next section.

1. Touch the Apps icon on the Home screen.

2. Touch the Play Store icon.

3. Touch Apps.

4. Touch the Search icon.

5. Type `play music`.

6. Touch the Google Play Music search result.

7. Touch Install.

8. Read the permissions the app requires and decide whether to accept them.

9. Touch Accept & Download. Your Galaxy Note II downloads the Play Music app and installs it.

Find Music

Now that the Play Music app is installed on your Galaxy Note II, you can add some music. One way to add music is to purchase it from Google.

1. Touch the Apps icon on the Home screen.

2. Touch the Play Music icon.

3. Touch the Market icon.

4. Touch to see new releases.

5. Swipe left to see a list of music genres.

6. Swipe right to see the Top Albums list. Swipe right again from the Top Albums list to see the Top Songs list.

7. Touch to search for music.

Purchase Music

After you find a song or album you want to purchase, use the following steps to make the purchase.

Free Music

Sometimes songs are offered for free. If a song is offered for free, you see the word Free instead of a price for the song. Even though the song is free, you still need to follow the steps outlined in this section; however, the price appears as 0.

1. Touch the price to the right of the song title or album.

2. Touch Accept & Buy.

3. Touch Listen to hear your song after the purchase is complete. You can also play the song or album from within the Play Music app.

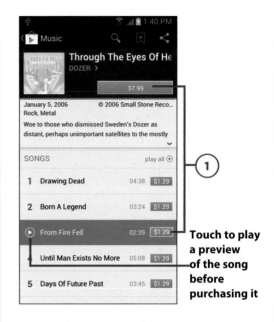

Touch to play a preview of the song before purchasing it

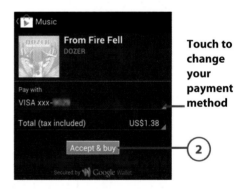

Touch to change your payment method

It's Not All Good

Cloud and Data Usage

Although cloud storage (where your music is stored on Google computers as opposed to on your Galaxy Note II) can be very beneficial, it does mean that anytime you listen to your music collection it is streamed over the network. If you are connected to Wi-Fi, this data streaming is free; however, if you are not connected to Wi-Fi, the data is streamed over the cellular network and counts against your data package. If you don't have a large or unlimited data package, you could incur large overage fees, so please be careful. Another disadvantage of streaming from the cloud is that when you have no cellular or Wi-Fi coverage, or you have very slow or spotty coverage, you are unable to access and listen to your music collection, or the songs stutter because of the poor connection. Be extra careful about this when traveling abroad because international data roaming charges are very expensive.

Add Your Existing Music to Google Music

You can upload up to 20,000 songs from Apple iTunes, Microsoft Windows Media Player, or music stored in folders on your computer to your Google Music cloud account by using the Google Music Manager app on your desktop computer. If you haven't already installed Google Music Manager, please follow the steps in the "Install Google Music Manager" section in the Prologue chapter, "Getting to Know Your Galaxy Note II."

1. Click (right-click for Windows) the Google Music Manager icon. On the Mac, this icon appears in the menu bar at the top of the screen. On Windows, the icon appears in the taskbar at the bottom of the screen.

2. Choose Preferences. (On Windows, choose Options.)

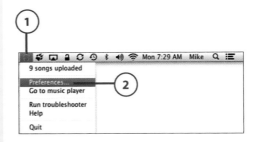

3. Click to upload new songs you have added to iTunes.

4. Click to upload the remainder of songs that have not yet uploaded.

5. Click to upload songs in certain playlists. This only works for iTunes or for Windows Media Player.

6. Choose the playlists to upload.

7. Click Upload after you have made your selections.

8. Click to allow Google Music Manager to automatically upload new songs added.

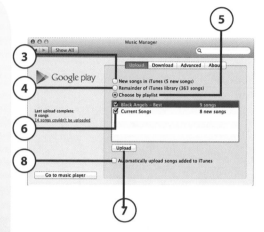

Automatic Upload

If you choose to have your music uploaded automatically in step 8, Google Music Manager continually monitors Apple iTunes, Microsoft Windows Media Player, or your Music folders to see if music has been added. If it finds new music, it automatically uploads it. After you install Google Music Manager, the app runs continuously, enabling it to detect music you add to iTunes, Windows Media Player, or your Music folders.

What If I Don't Have iTunes or Windows Media Player?

If you don't have or don't use Apple iTunes or Microsoft Windows Media Player to store and play your music, Google Music Manager can use folders on your computer to upload music from. Click the Advanced tab, click Change, and select either Music Folder, to use the folder on your computer called Music, or Other Folders to let you choose folders where you store your music. Click Add Folder to add a new folder to the list.

Can I Download Music to My Computer?

You can download your entire music collection from Google Music to your computer, or just download music you have purchased on your Galaxy Note II. While in Google Music Manager Preferences, click Download.

Use the Music Application

Now that you have some music synchronized to Google Music, it's time to take a look at the Google Music app on your Galaxy Note II.

1. Touch the Apps icon on the Home screen.

2. Touch the Play Music icon on the Apps screen.

Swiping Between Tabs

As you use the following steps, instead of touching items such as Albums and Artists in the Navigation bar, you can swipe left and right to move between these categories instead.

3. Touch Recent in the Navigation bar to display music you have recently added or played.

4. Touch Shuffle All to shuffle the songs into a random order and start one playing.

5. Touch an album to display its contents. You can then touch a song to start it playing.

6. Touch Playlists in the Navigation bar to display the playlists you have synchronized to your Galaxy Note II. Read more about how to do that later in the chapter.

7. Touch a playlist to display its contents.

8. Touch a song in the playlist to start it playing.

9. Touch to return to the Playlists screen. From here, you can navigate to another category.

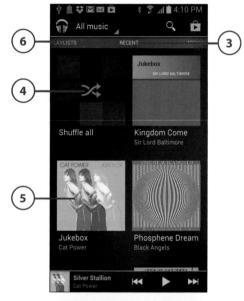

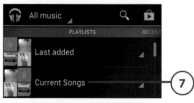

10. Swipe right or touch Artists in the Navigation bar to display your music listed by artists.

11. Touch an artist's name to show albums by that artist.

12. Touch an album to display the songs it contains. You can then touch a song to play it.

13. Swipe right or touch Songs to display the list of songs by title. This view shows all songs by all artists.

14. Touch a song to play it.

15. Swipe right or touch Genres to display the list of genres for your music.

16. Touch a genre to display the albums it contains.

17. Touch an album to display its contents. You can then tap a song to start it playing.

18. Touch to get music from the Play Store.

19. Touch to search for music in your collection.

What's currently
playing

Control Playback

While playing music, you can control both how the music plays and the selection of music that plays.

1. If all the controls shown here do not appear on screen, touch the album picture to display the controls. The Play Music app automatically hides the controls after a few seconds of you not using them.

2. Touch once to go back to the start of the current song. Touch again to skip back to the previous song in the album, playlist, or shuffle.

3. Touch to skip ahead to the next song in the album, playlist, or shuffle.

4. Touch to pause the song. The button turns into the Play button when a song is paused. Touch again to resume playing a paused song.

5. Touch to indicate you like the song. The thumbs-up icon turns blue to indicate you have applied the rating. Touch again to remove the rating. The Google Music app also adds the song to the "Thumbs Up" playlist.

6. Touch to indicate you do not like the song. The thumbs-down icon turns blue to indicate you have applied the rating. Touch again to remove the rating.

7. Touch and drag to change the position in the song.

8. Touch to enable or disable song shuffling. When Shuffle is enabled, songs in the current playlist, album, or song list are randomly played.

9. Touch to display the list of songs in the album. The list shows only the songs you have purchased or downloaded.

10. Touch to enable repeating. Touch once to repeat all songs, touch again to repeat the current song only, and touch a third time to disable repeating.

11. Touch a song to play it.

12. Touch to display a menu of actions you can take with the song.

13. Touch to play the song now.

14. Touch to play the song next, after the current song finishes.

15. Touch to make an instant mix based on the song.

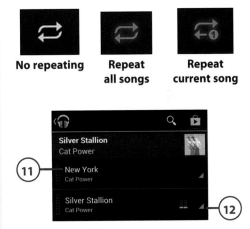

No repeating   Repeat all songs   Repeat current song

What Is an Instant Mix?

If you are playing a song and choose to create an instant mix as mentioned in step 15, the Google Music app creates a new playlist and adds songs to it that are similar to the one you are currently playing. The name of the playlist is the name of the current song plus the word *mix*. For example, if you are playing the song "Trail" and choose to create an instant mix, the playlist is called "Trail Mix."

16. Touch to add the song to an existing playlist or create a new playlist using this song.

17. Touch to remove the song from the play queue.

18. Touch to locate more songs by the artist.

19. Touch to shop for more songs by the artist.

20. Touch to delete the song from your library on the Galaxy Note II.

21. Touch to display the album's art instead of the song list.

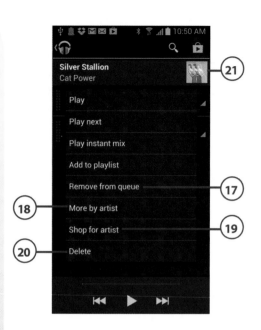

Work and Listen to Music

You don't have to keep the Play Music app displayed while you are playing music. Instead, you can switch back to the Home screen and run any other app but still have the ability to control the music.

1. Pull down the Notification bar.

2. Touch to pause the song.

3. Touch to skip ahead to the next song in the list, album, or playlist.

4. Touch the song title to open the Google Music app for more control.

5. Touch to stop playing the song and remove the playback control from the Notification bar.

What If I Get a Call?

If someone calls you while you are listening to music, your Galaxy Note II pauses the music and displays the regular incoming call screen. After you hang up, the music continues playing.

Work with Playlists

Playlists can be a great way of listening to music, enabling you to group together related songs or simply those you want to hear in a particular sequence. On your Galaxy Note II, you can create new playlists, add songs to existing playlists, rename playlists, and change the order of the songs they contain.

Create a New Playlist on Your Galaxy Note II

1. Using the techniques described earlier in this chapter, navigate to a song you want to add to the new playlist.

2. Touch to open the dialog of actions. You can also touch and hold the song name to open the dialog.

3. Touch Add to Playlist.

4. Touch New Playlist.

5. Type the name for the new playlist.

6. Touch OK.

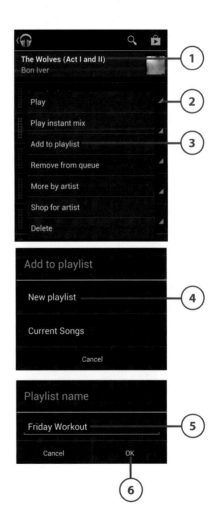

Add a Song to an Existing Playlist

1. Using the techniques described earlier in this chapter, navigate to a song you want to add to the new playlist.

2. Touch to open the dialog of actions. You can also touch and hold the song name to open the dialog.

3. Touch Add to Playlist.

4. Touch the playlist you want to add the song to.

Rename a Playlist

1. Touch to open the dialog of actions.

2. Touch Rename.

Deleting a Playlist

When you no longer need a playlist, delete it. On the Playlists screen, touch and hold the playlist to display the dialog of actions and then touch Delete. In the confirmation dialog, touch OK.

3. Type the new name for the playlist.

4. Touch Rename.

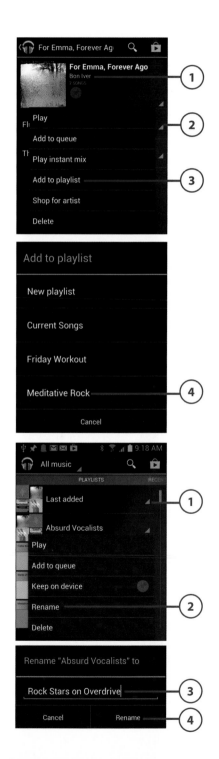

Rearrange the Songs in a Playlist

1. Touch a playlist to show the songs in it.

2. Touch and hold the dotted handle to the left of the song you want to move. Drag the song up or down until it is in the right place and then release it.

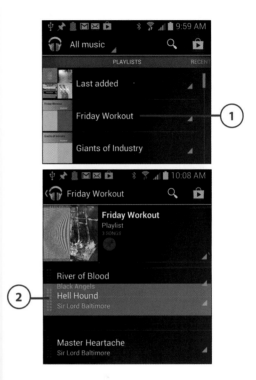

Listen to Music with No Wireless Coverage

If you use Google Music and store your music online, your Galaxy Note II streams the music over the cellular or Wi-Fi network when you play the music. If you know you are going to be without a signal but still want to listen to your music, you need to store it on your Galaxy Note II.

1. Using the techniques discussed earlier in this chapter, go to the music you want to store on your Galaxy Note II.

2. Touch and hold the item to display the dialog of actions.

3. Touch Keep on Device.

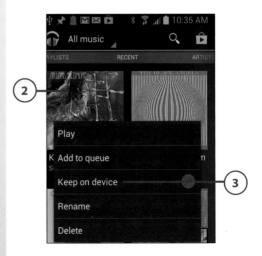

SYNCHRONIZE MUSIC AND OTHER MEDIA USING A USB CABLE

If you don't use Google Music, or Google Music is not available in your country, you can synchronize music and other media using a USB cable or Wi-Fi. You can use Kies, the program that Samsung provides for managing its phones and tablets, or another app such as doubleTwist (http://www. doubletwist.com). Alternatively, you can connect your Galaxy Note II via USB and access its file system using Windows Explorer.

ENJOY MUSIC ON YOUR GALAXY NOTE II USING OTHER APPS

As you have seen so far in this chapter, Google's Play Music app is easy to use and enables you to access the music you store in your Google account. But you will probably also want to explore the other apps most Galaxy Note II models include for enjoying music.

The Music Hub app enables you to upload your music collection to Samsung's online service and play it back from there. You can also buy music from the 19 million songs the Music Hub sells. Music Hub is a subscription service.

The Music Player app is an easy-to-use app for playing back music. Music Player includes features such as an equalizer for adjusting the sound and Music Square, which lets you select music by touching the appropriate point on a grid with the axes Exciting, Joyful, Passionate, and Calm.

Playing and Sharing Videos

The Gallery app enables you to view pictures and video; you can also share pictures and video with people on Facebook, or via MMS, Bluetooth, YouTube, and email. This section explains how you can view and share videos. Later in this chapter, you find out how to take pictures and share them.

1. Touch the Gallery icon to launch the Gallery app.

2. Touch an album to open it, revealing the pictures and videos it contains.

3. Touch a video to start it playing. Videos have a little Play icon on them.

4. Touch the screen while the video is playing to reveal the video controls. If you do not use the controls, they disappear after a few seconds.

5. Touch to pause or unpause the video.

6. Drag the slider to scrub quickly forward and backward.

7. Touch to skip to the end of the video.

8. Touch to return to the beginning of the video.

9. Touch to switch between viewing the video full screen and viewing it as best fits the Galaxy Note II's screen.

Changing the Orientation for a Video

When watching a video shot in landscape orientation, rotate your Galaxy Note II from portrait orientation to landscape orientation so you can enjoy the video full screen.

10. Touch to display the video in a pop-up window. You can then switch to another screen and continue to watch the video as you work or play.

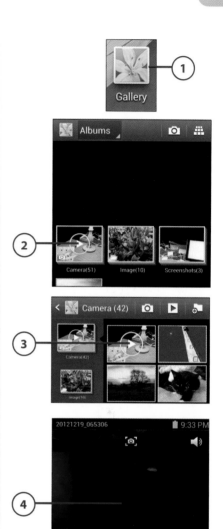

11. Touch to pause or restart the video. When you touch, an X appears in the upper-right corner.

12. Touch to close the pop-up video window.

Share Videos

From the Gallery app, you can share small videos with other people.

1. Touch and hold the video you want to share. After a moment, a green check mark appears on the video.

2. Touch to open the Share Via dialog.

3. Scroll up if necessary to display other methods of sharing.

4. Touch a method for sharing the video.

Sharing Only Small Videos

It is best to share only small videos from your Galaxy Note II. Even when using email, try to share videos no larger than 10MB, which is only two or three minutes of high-quality video. Otherwise, your videos will be too large to transfer successfully.

Bluetooth Sharing Might Fail

Many phones do not accept incoming Bluetooth files, but devices like computers do. Even on computers, the recipient must configure her Bluetooth configuration to accept incoming files.

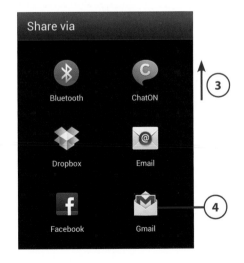

Share a Video on YouTube

If you have not previously set up your YouTube account on your Galaxy Note II, you are prompted to do so before you can upload your video.

1. Enter the title of your video.

2. Enter a description of your video.

3. Select whether to make your video public for everyone to see or whether to keep it private.

Sharing a YouTube Video Only with Specific People

As well as the Public setting and the Private setting, the Privacy pop-up list provides an Unlisted setting. Choose Unlisted when you need to share the video with some people but not with everyone. The video then does not appear in the public view of your YouTube account, but you can send the URL for the video to anyone you want to view it.

4. Enter any tags for your video. Tags are keywords that help people find videos by searching.

5. Touch Upload.

Share Video on Facebook

If you have not previously set up a Facebook account on your Galaxy Note II, you are prompted to do so before you can upload your video.

1. Enter a description of your video.

2. Touch Post.

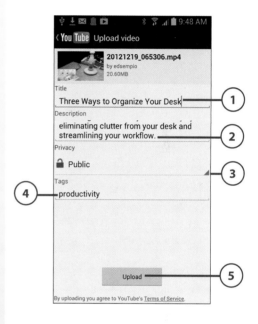

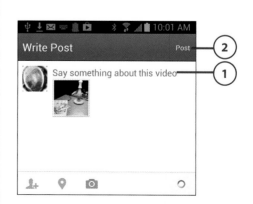

Delete Videos

1. Touch and hold the video you want to share. After a moment, a green check mark appears on the video.

2. Touch to delete the video.

3. Touch OK.

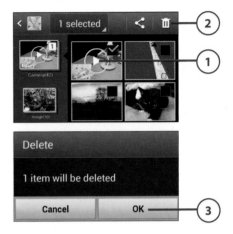

Taking Photos and Videos with the Camera App

The Camera app enables you to take still photos and record videos.

Take Photos

1. Touch to launch the Camera app.

2. Make sure the switch is set to the still camera position. If it isn't, slide the switch right to the still camera position to switch from the video camera to the still camera.

3. Touch to switch from the rear camera to the front camera so you can take photos of yourself. The front camera is lower resolution than the rear camera, but it works well for capturing candid self-portraits.

4. Touch to take a photo.

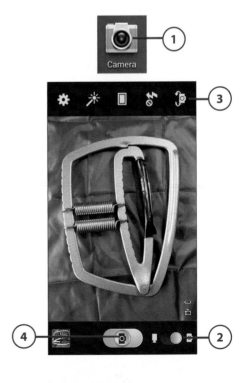

Taking a Burst of Photos

Instead of taking a single shot, the Camera app can take a burst of photos. This feature is great when you do not have time to compose your photo perfectly or your subject is moving. To take a burst of photos, touch and hold the shutter release.

Change Camera Settings

You can get good photos by using your Galaxy Note II as a point-and-shoot camera, as described in the previous section. But you can get photos by changing settings to harness the full power of the Camera app.

Touch and hold to take a burst of photos

1. Touch to change the flash setting among Off, On, and Auto Flash.

Making the Most of the Flash

Choose the Off setting for the flash when you need to take photos where the flash would be disruptive. Choose the On setting when you need to light the foreground of a shot even though the rest of the scene is amply lit—for example, to light your subject's face in front of a bright background. Choose the Auto setting for general use.

2. Touch to change the Shooting mode setting among Single Shot, Best Photo, Best Faces, Face Detection, Panorama, Share Shot, HDR, Buddy Photo Share, Beauty, Smile Shot, and Low Light.

Sharing Your Photos as You Take Them

Share Shot is a feature for sharing photos with other Samsung phones via a Wi-Fi Direct network. After you turn on Share Shot, your Galaxy Note II immediately shares photos you take to participating phones.

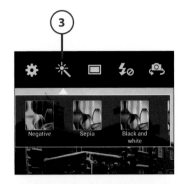

3. Touch to apply an effect such as Negative (reversed colors), Sepia, or Black and White to the photos you take. Choose No Effect when you want to turn off the effect.

4. Touch to choose further settings, such as Anti-Shake, GPS Tag, Resolution, and White Balance. These settings include the ones whose shortcuts appear at the top of the screen.

Adjusting the Light Metering for Your Photos

By default, your Galaxy Note II uses center-weighted light metering, giving most importance to the light conditions in the center of the photo. Open the Metering dialog and choose Spot instead to base the light metering on the spot you touch in the frame. Choose Matrix to base the metering from samples across the entire frame.

Touch to choose light metering

Touch the metering type

USING THE SHOOTING MODE SETTINGS

Your Galaxy Note II's Camera app gives you a wide choice of shooting modes. By choosing the right mode for the type of photos you are taking, you improve your chances of getting high-quality pictures.

Some of the shooting modes are straightforward: Choose Single Shot for taking regular photos one at a time; choose Panorama when you need to stitch together a sequence of photos into a panorama photo; or choose Low Light to counter problems that occur when taking photos in dim conditions, such as camera shake.

Other shooting modes have less obvious names but can be equally useful. Choose Best Photo to have the Camera app take a rapid burst of eight photos and walk you through choosing the best-looking one. Choose Best Faces to take five shots at a slightly slower pace and then choose the best shot or most amusing expression.

Choose Buddy Photo Share to share photos with your buddies based on the faces you identify in them. For example, if you tag a face as being Chris Smith, you can then touch the Email button next to the tag to send that photo to Chris Smith.

Choose Smile Shot when you want to take close-up shots of someone smiling. When you touch the shutter release, the Camera app beeps to signal it's ready, but it takes the photo only when the subject smiles or grimaces.

View the Photos You Take

After taking photos, you can quickly view the photos you have taken, mark them as favorites, share them with other people, or simply delete them.

1. Touch to view the last photo you took.

Zooming In and Out on Your Photos

When viewing a photo, you can zoom in by placing two fingers on the screen and pinching outward or by double-tapping on the area you want to expand. Pinch inward or double-tap again to zoom back out.

2. Touch to display the onscreen controls and the row of thumbnails. They disappear after a few seconds of not being used.

3. Touch to mark the photo as a favorite.

4. Touch a thumbnail to display its photo; scroll the thumbnails first if necessary. You can also swipe left from the photo displayed; after that, you can swipe either left or right.

5. Touch to share the photo. In the Share Via dialog, touch the means of sharing, and then provide any information needed—for example, the recipient for a photo you share via email.

6. Touch to delete the photo and then touch OK in the confirmation dialog.

7. Touch to return to the Camera app.

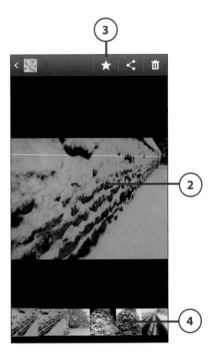

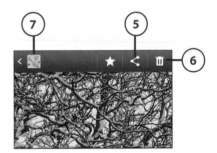

Record Videos with the Camera App

Recording videos with the Camera app is even easier than taking still photos because there are fewer options to choose.

1. Touch to launch the Camera app.

2. Slide the switch from the still camera position to the video camera position.

3. Touch to start recording video. Touch the icon again to stop recording.

Using Automatic and Manual Focusing

While the Camera app is recording video, it automatically adjusts the focus for the object in the center of the screen. If you need to focus on another part of the screen, touch it.

Change Video Settings

Before you record a video, you can change the video settings to control how the Camera app records the video.

1. Touch to switch from the rear camera to the front camera. Touch again to switch back.

2. Touch to turn the flash on or off.

3. Touch to display the Recording Mode dialog and then touch Normal, Limit for MMS, Slow Motion, or Fast Motion, as needed.

4. Touch to apply effects—such as Black and White, Cartoonify, or Washed Out—to the video you shoot.

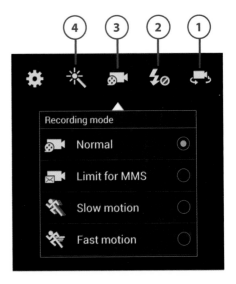

5. Touch to see the full list of video settings and then scroll up or down as needed.

6. Touch a setting to display options for it and then touch the option you want.

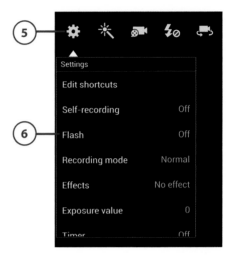

USING THE MOST HELPFUL SETTINGS

>>>Go Further

Of the Camera app's settings for video, five tend to be most helpful:

- Touch Timer to start recording after a delay of 2, 5, or 10 seconds.

- Touch Exposure to increase or decrease the exposure—for example, increase the exposure when filming against a bright background.

- Touch White Balance to change the white balance among Auto, Daylight, Cloudy, Incandescent, and Fluorescent.

- Touch Guidelines to turn on a grid of lines that help you compose your shots and orient the camera.

- Touch Anti-Shake to turn on stabilization when you are filming by hand rather than using a tripod.

Enjoying Videos with the YouTube App

Your Galaxy Note II comes with a YouTube app that enables you to find and watch videos, rate them, add them to your favorites, and share links with other people. The app even enables you to upload your own videos to YouTube.

Meet the YouTube Main Screen

1. Touch the YouTube icon to launch the YouTube app.

2. Touch to search YouTube using keywords.

3. Touch your account name to see your account details.

4. Touch to see your YouTube channel (if you have one). Your channel contains the videos you have uploaded to YouTube.

5. Touch a category in the From YouTube list to browse videos by category.

6. Swipe left to close the Account pane and browse the videos in your chosen category full screen.

7. Touch a video to see more information about it and play it.

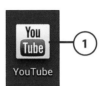

Play a Video

While playing a YouTube video, you can rate the video, read comments about it, or share it with other people.

1. Touch the video to display the onscreen controls for a few seconds.

2. Touch to start or pause the video.

Viewing a Video Full Screen

Rotate your Galaxy Note II into Landscape mode to see the video full screen. Return your Galaxy Note II to Portrait mode to restore the previous view.

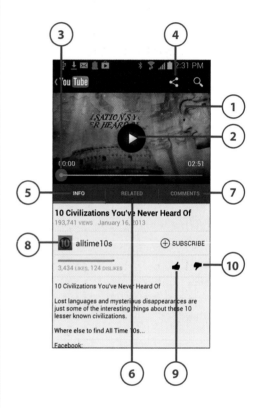

3. Drag to scrub forward or backward through the video.

4. Touch to share the video's link (its URL) via apps such as Gmail, Facebook, or Twitter.

5. Touch to see information about the video, including who uploaded it, the video title, description, and how many times it has been viewed.

6. Touch to see YouTube videos that are related to the video you are watching. YouTube finds videos that are related because of content and keywords.

7. Touch to comment on the video you are watching and read other people's comments.

8. Touch to see the YouTube channel of the person who uploaded the video.

9. Touch to like the video.

10. Touch to dislike the video.

11. Touch the Menu button to display the menu, which contains further options.

12. Touch to add the video to your Watch Later list, your YouTube Favorites list, or another playlist.

13. Touch to like the video.

14. Touch to dislike the video.

15. Touch to add the video to your YouTube TV list.

16. Touch to copy the YouTube video link to the Galaxy Note II's clipboard. You can then paste it into text in any app—for example, email.

17. Touch to flag the video as inappropriate.

18. Touch to check or change your YouTube settings. See the next section for details.

19. Touch to send feedback to YouTube, either about this video or in general.

20. Touch to open your browser to help screens on using YouTube.

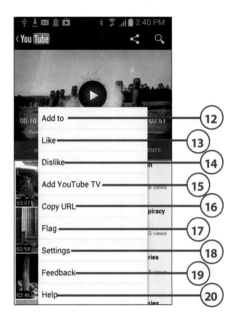

Change YouTube Settings

To get more out of YouTube, you might want to change your settings. Your options include choosing whether to watch high-quality videos on cellular connections, clearing your YouTube search history, and enabling the preloading of items on your subscriptions list or your Watch Later list.

1. From within the YouTube app, touch the Menu button.

2. Touch Settings.

3. Touch General.

4. Touch to enable or disable always starting videos in High Quality mode. The video might take longer to start playing, and it uses more data in High Quality mode.

5. Touch to set the size of the font used when a video has captions.

6. Touch to choose when your Galaxy Note II uploads videos to YouTube. Your choices are Only When on Wi-Fi, and On Any Network.

7. Touch to return to the main Settings screen.

8. Touch Search.

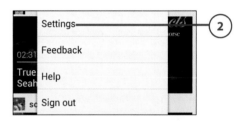

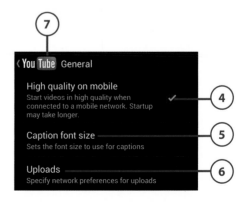

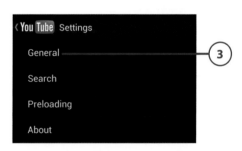

9. Touch to clear your YouTube search history.

10. Touch to set the types of videos that are displayed when you search. If you set this setting to Don't Filter, no videos are filtered out based on content.

11. Touch to return to the main Settings screen.

12. Touch Preloading.

13. Touch to enable or disable preloading of videos to which you have subscribed. Preloading videos enables you to start watching them sooner on slow networks, but storing the files takes up space on your Galaxy Note II.

14. Touch to enable or disable preloading of videos you have added to your Watch Later list.

15. Touch to return to the main Settings screen.

16. Touch the YouTube button to return to the YouTube app.

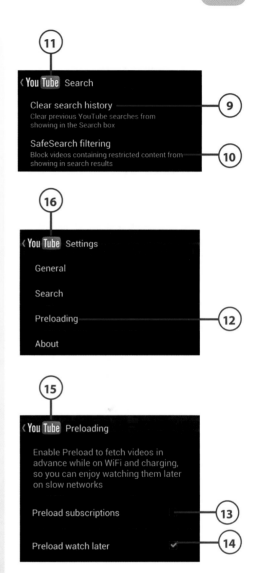

Upload a Video to YouTube from the YouTube App

After you create your own channel, you can easily upload your videos to YouTube straight from the YouTube app.

1. On the main YouTube screen, touch to start uploading a video.

2. In the Choose Video to Upload dialog, touch the source of the video. For example, touch Gallery.

3. Touch the video you want to upload.

4. On the Upload Video screen, enter the information for the video, as discussed earlier in this chapter, and then touch Upload.

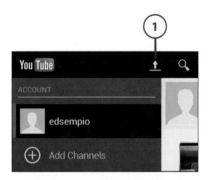

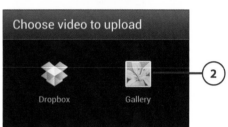

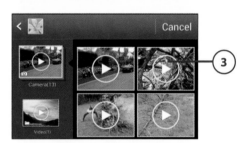

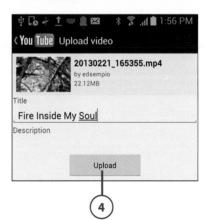

Browse quickly through thumb-nails of magazine pages

In this chapter, you discover your Galaxy Note II's capabilities for carrying and displaying books and magazines. Topics include the following:

→ Reading books with the Play Books app
→ Installing and using Amazon's Kindle app
→ Finding free e-books online
→ Reading magazines with Google Play Magazines

Books and Magazines

With its large, bright screen, your Galaxy Note II is great for reading books and magazines. You can load an entire library and newsstand onto your Galaxy Note II, take the device with you anywhere, and read to your heart's content.

Reading Books with Play Books and Kindle

Books are perfect media for your Galaxy Note II because their file sizes are mostly small but they deliver long-lasting entertainment. Your Galaxy Note II likely comes with one or more apps for reading books, but you will probably want to supplement them with other apps, such as the free Kindle app from Amazon.

Open the Play Books App and Meet Your Library

Google's Play Books app provides straightforward reading capabilities and ties in to the Books area of Google's Play Store, from which you can buy many books and download others for free.

1. On the Apps screen, touch Play Books.

2. Touch to open a book that is already in your library. Depending on where you bought your Galaxy Note II, it might include several public-domain books as samples. If your library is empty, you can get books from the Play Store.

3. A gray pin indicates the book is stored online rather than on your Galaxy Note II. Touch a gray pin to make the book available offline.

4. A blue pin indicates the book is available offline because it is stored on your Galaxy Note II.

5. Touch to go to the Books section of the Play Store to buy books or download free books.

6. Touch to search your library for books by keyword. Searching is useful when you have built up a large library. When your library contains only a few books, you can browse through them easily.

7. Touch the Menu button.

8. Touch View as Carousel to switch the book list to Carousel view.

9. In Carousel view, swipe left or right to display other books.

10. Touch a book to open it.

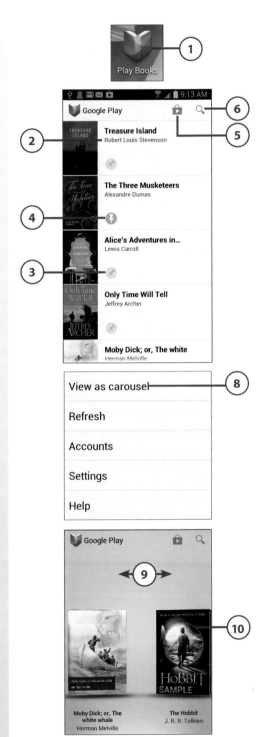

Get Books from the Play Store

1. In the Play Books app, touch the Play Store icon to display the Books area of the Play Store. The Featured list appears first.

2. Touch to search for books.

3. Touch to see the list of top-selling books.

4. Touch a featured book or a recommended book to see its details.

5. Touch a featured category to see the list of books it contains.

6. Touch to display the list of categories. You can also swipe right to display the list of categories.

7. Touch the category you want to display. The Featured list for the category appears first.

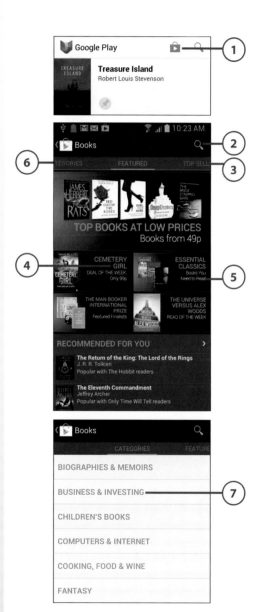

8. Swipe up to see more of the list.

9. Touch or swipe left to see the New Arrivals list for the category.

10. Touch a book to display its details.

11. Touch to add the book to your wish list.

12. Touch to share the book with others via Facebook, Twitter, Gmail, Messaging, or another means of sharing.

13. Touch Rate & Review to rate or review the book. You would normally do this after reading the book, but many raters and reviewers skip the reading step.

14. Touch to expand the description.

15. Swipe up to read the reviews and to see the Users Also Viewed list of books that may interest you.

16. Touch Free Sample to download a free sample of the book. Reading the sample can be a great way to decide whether to spend the money on the book. Android downloads the book and displays its first page in the Google Books app.

Buying Books from the Play Store

To buy a book from the Play Store, you must either add a credit card to your Google account or redeem a voucher. When you go to buy a book, the Play Store app prompts you to add a credit card and walks you through the steps for adding it.

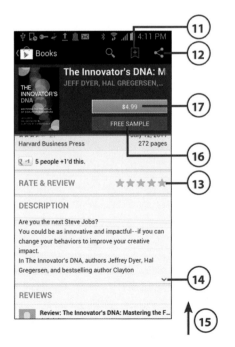

17. Touch the price button to buy the book, and then follow through the payment process on the next screen. If the book is free, touch the Open button. Android downloads the book and displays its first page in Google Books.

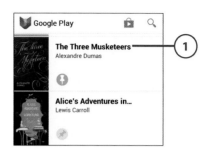

Finding Free E-Books Online

Apart from buying e-books online at Google's Play Store or other stores such as Amazon (www.amazon.com) and Barnes & Noble (www.barnesandnoble.com), you can find many books for free. Most online stores offer some free e-books, especially out-of-copyright classics, so it is worth browsing the Free lists. Other good sources of free e-books include ManyBooks.net (www.manybooks.net) and Project Gutenberg (www.gutenberg.org).

Read Books with the Play Books App

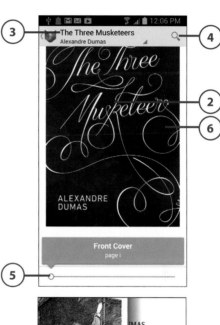

1. On the opening screen of the Play Books app, touch the book you want to open. The cover appears if this is the first time you have opened the book. Otherwise, the page at which you last left the book appears.

2. Touch the middle of the screen to display the navigation controls at the top and bottom of the screen. The controls remain onscreen for a few seconds and then disappear if you do not use them. You can make them disappear more quickly by touching the screen again.

3. Touch to display an information panel about the book.

4. Touch to search within the book for specific text.

5. Drag to move quickly through the book.

6. Touch the right side of the screen or drag left to turn the page forward. Dragging lets you turn the page partway to peek ahead.

7. Touch the left side of the screen or drag right to turn the page back.

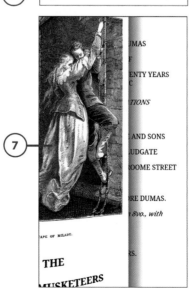

Choose Options for the Play Books App

You can configure the Play Books app to make it work your way. Options include switching between flowing text and the original pages of the book, adding bookmarks, and having your Galaxy Note II read aloud to you.

1. In the Play Books app, touch the Menu button.

2. Touch to display the book's table of contents. From here, you can touch the section to which you want to jump.

3. Touch to display the book's original pages instead of the flowing text. When you want to switch back, touch the Menu button and then touch Flowing text. Even though your Galaxy Note II has a large screen, the original pages are usually too small for easy reading.

4. Touch to display the book's page in the Play Store.

5. Touch to share the book's URL on the Play Store via Facebook, Gmail, Twitter, or another means of sharing.

6. Touch to enable or disable storing the book on your Galaxy Note II.

7. Touch to add a bookmark to the current page. To remove the bookmark, go to the page, touch the Menu button, and then touch Remove Bookmark.

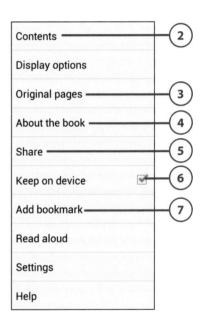

8. Touch Read Aloud to start the Play Books app reading aloud to you from the beginning of the first paragraph that starts on this page. To stop the reading, touch the Menu button, and then touch Stop Reading Aloud.

9. Touch to display the Settings screen.

What Settings Does the Play Books App Offer?

The Play Books app has only two settings. Check the Download Over Wi-Fi Only box if you want to prevent Play Books from downloading books over your cellular connection. Check the Automatically Read Aloud box if you want Play Books to start reading aloud when you relaunch the app after leaving it reading aloud.

10. Touch to get help on the Play Books app.

11. Touch to open the Display Options panel.

12. Touch to choose between the Day theme and the Night theme. The Day theme uses black text on a white background, whereas the Night theme uses white text on a black background.

13. Touch to change the typeface used.

14. Touch to change the text alignment. The choices are Default, Left, and Justify.

15. Touch to enable or disable automatic brightness.

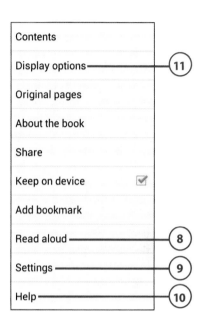

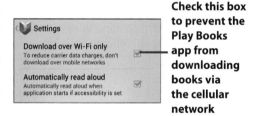

Check this box to prevent the Play Books app from downloading books via the cellular network

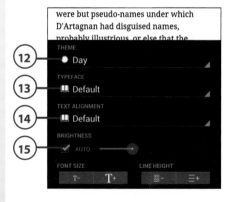

16. Drag to adjust the brightness manually.

17. Touch to decrease the font size.

18. Touch to increase the font size.

19. Touch to decrease the spacing between lines.

20. Touch to increase the spacing between lines.

21. Touch the book page to close the Display Options panel.

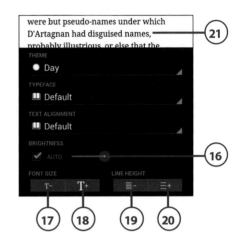

Install the Kindle App

Google's Play Store has a good selection of books, but if you want to buy or download books from Amazon's vast bookstore, you need to use the Kindle app instead.

Installing the Kindle App

If the Kindle app is not already installed on your Galaxy Note II, you need to install it from the Play Store. Touch Play Store on the Apps screen, touch Apps on the Google Play screen, touch the Search icon, and type **kindle**. Touch the Kindle result and then touch Install.

Touch to search

Touch to install

Register the Kindle App

1. On the Apps screen, touch the Amazon Kindle icon. The first time you run the Kindle app, it displays the registration screen.

2. Type your email address.

Creating an Amazon Account

To buy books or download free books from Amazon, you must have an Amazon account. If you do not have one, touch the Don't Have an Amazon Account? button on the Kindle registration screen and then follow through the screens to create an account.

3. Touch and type your Amazon password.

4. Touch Register. The Kindle app registers your account and then displays its Home screen.

5. Touch On Device to see the list of books stored on your Galaxy Note II.

6. Touch Archive to see the list of books you have previously purchased or downloaded for free from Amazon. From here, you can touch a book to download it to your Galaxy Note II.

7. Touch to go to the Amazon store to buy books.

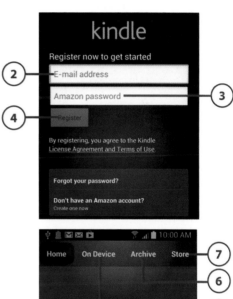

Read a Book with the Kindle App

1. In the Kindle app, touch On Device to display the On Device screen.

Reaching the On Device Screen from a Book

If you currently have a book open in the Kindle app, touch the Back button to go back to the main screens and then touch On Device. Alternatively, touch the Menu button, touch Home to display the Kindle Home screen, and then touch On Device.

2. Touch the book you want to open.

3. Touch the middle of the screen to display the title and location bar. Touch again to hide these items.

4. Drag the slider to change the location in the book.

5. Touch the right side of the screen to display the next page. You can also display the next page by dragging or swiping left.

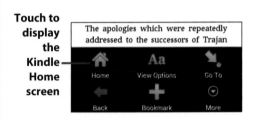

Touch to display the Kindle Home screen

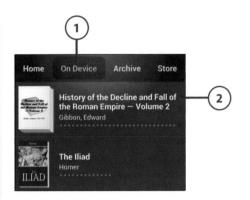

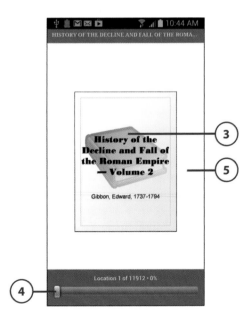

6. Touch the left side of the screen, or drag or swipe right, to move back a page.

7. Touch the Menu button to display the menu.

8. Touch Bookmark to bookmark the current page.

9. Touch Go To to display the Go To dialog.

10. Touch to display the cover.

11. Touch to display the table of contents. This command is unavailable if the book has no table of contents.

12. Touch to go to the beginning of the text, after the cover.

13. Touch to go to a page by number. If the book does not have page numbers, this command is unavailable.

14. Touch to go to a location. The locations are numbered divisions of the text. You can see the number of the current location by touching the middle of the screen and looking at the Location slider. But unless you know the number of the location to which you want to go, this command is of little use.

15. Touch to display your notes and bookmarks. From there, you can touch one of your bookmarks to go to the bookmarked page.

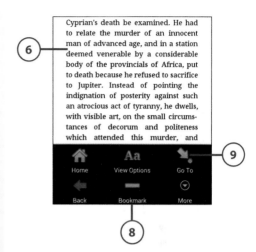

Choose View Options for the Kindle App

To make your books easy to read, you can choose view options for them.

1. With a book open in the Kindle app, touch the Menu button.

2. Touch View Options.

3. Touch to decrease the font size.

4. Touch to increase the font size.

5. Touch to adjust the space between lines.

6. Touch to adjust the margin width.

7. Touch to choose the color scheme: White, Sepia, or Black.

8. Drag to adjust the brightness.

9. Touch the document to close the View Options panel.

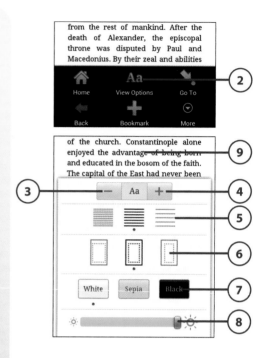

EXPLORE OTHER BOOK READERS

>>>Go Further

Between them, the Play Books app and the Kindle app give you access to a phenomenal range of books. But there are many other book readers you might want to explore to give yourself access to other bookstores and other books. In particular, the Aldiko app, the Kobo app, and the Nook app are worth trying. You can get each of these apps from the Play Store for free. The Nook app ties into Barnes & Noble's online bookstore.

Reading Magazines with Play Magazines

Your Galaxy Note II includes Google's Play Magazines app, which gives you access to a wide range of magazines.

Exploring Other Magazine Apps

If the Play Magazines app does not deliver the content you need, or does not otherwise suit you, explore other magazine apps such as PressReader and Zinio. You can download both these apps for free from the Apps section of the Play Store.

Open the Play Magazines App and Choose Your Magazines

1. On the Apps screen, touch Play Magazines. Your current magazine subscriptions appear as a cascading stack.

2. Touch a magazine to open it. See the next task for information about reading magazines.

3. Drag left to display another magazine in the stack.

4. Touch the Play Store icon to display the Magazines section of the Play Store.

5. Touch to see the list of top-selling magazines.

6. Touch a featured magazine or a recommended magazine to see its details.

7. Touch a featured category to see the list of magazines it contains.

8. Touch to display the list of categories. You can also swipe right to display the list of categories.

9. Touch the category you want to display.

10. Swipe up to see more of the list.

11. Touch or swipe left to see the New Arrivals list for the category.

12. Touch a magazine to display its details.

13. Touch to add the magazine to your wish list.

14. Touch to share the magazine with others via Facebook, Twitter, Gmail, Messaging, or another means of sharing.

15. Touch Rate & Review to rate or review the magazine.

16. Swipe up to read the reviews and to see the Similar Magazines list, which might contain magazines that interest you. At the bottom of the screen, you also find the Back Issues list.

17. Touch Subscribe to start a 30-day trial subscription to the magazine, followed by a paid subscription if you do not cancel it. You can choose between a yearly subscription and a monthly subscription. Android downloads the magazine and displays its first page in the Google Magazines app.

18. Touch the price button to buy the magazine, and then follow through the payment process on the next screen. If the magazine is free, touch the Open button. Android downloads the magazine and displays its first page in Google Magazines.

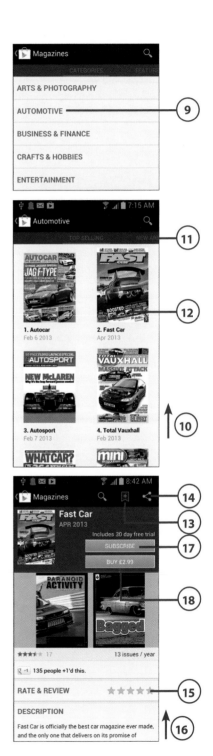

Read a Magazine with the Play Magazines App

1. On the opening screen of the Play Magazines app, touch the magazine you want to open. The cover appears if this is the first time you have opened the magazine. Otherwise, the page at which you last left the magazine appears.

2. Touch the middle of the screen to display the navigation controls at the top and bottom of the screen. The controls remain onscreen for a few seconds and then disappear if you do not use them. You can make them disappear more quickly by touching the screen again.

3. Touch to display a text-only version of the magazine. The text-only version can be much easier to read on your Galaxy Note II's screen, but only some magazines have a text-only version.

4. Drag to scroll through the pages.

5. Touch to display the next page.

6. Touch a page's thumbnail to display that page.

7. Touch to display a table of contents.

8. Touch an article to display the page that contains it.

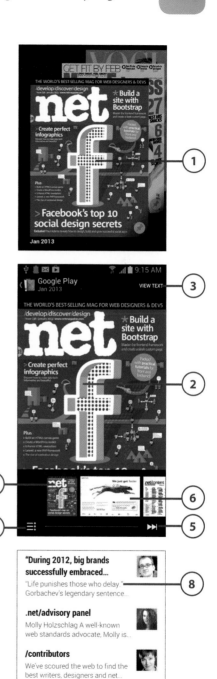

9. Double-tap or pinch outward with two fingers to zoom the page as needed.

10. Swipe left to display the next page or right to display the previous page.

Choose Options for the Play Magazines App

The Play Magazines app has several settings you can choose to control when it downloads magazines and when it notifies you about new issues. You can also change the account you use to pay for Play Magazines.

1. From the opening screen in the Play Magazines app, touch the Menu button.

2. Touch Settings.

3. Touch to change the account used for Play Magazines.

4. Touch to enable or disable automatic downloading of all your magazine purchases and subscriptions.

5. Touch to enable or disable limiting magazine downloads to when your Galaxy Note II has a Wi-Fi connection. Because magazine files can be relatively large, checking this box is a good idea if your cellular data plan is limited.

6. Touch to allow or prevent Play Magazines from showing you notifications about new issues.

7. Touch to return to the opening screen.

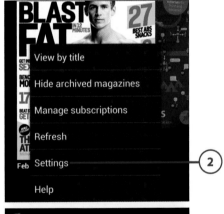

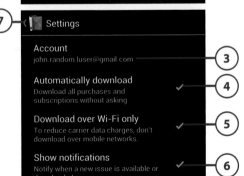

BROWSE NEWS AND SOCIAL NETWORKS WITH FLIPBOARD

If you enjoy both social networking and reading from various magazines and websites, try the Flipboard app. Your Galaxy Note II may already have Flipboard installed; if not, launch the Play Store app, search for Flipboard, and download it for free.

Flipboard gives you customizable access to stories drawn from various online publications. You can also add your newsfeed from Facebook and your timeline from Twitter, enabling you to browse both international and interpersonal news in a single app.

Flip the top down to refresh the display

Touch a story to display it

Flip the bottom up to display the next page

Search for apps

Browse for apps

In this chapter, you find out how to purchase and use Android apps on your Galaxy Note II. Topics include the following:

→ Finding apps with Google Play
→ Purchasing apps
→ Keeping apps up to date

Working with Android Apps

Your Galaxy Note II comes with enough apps to make it a worthy smartphone. However, wouldn't it be great to play games, update your Facebook and Twitter statuses, or even keep a grocery list? Well, finding these types of apps is what Google Play is for. Read on to learn about finding, purchasing, and maintaining apps.

What Happened to Android Market?
In 2012, Google updated the functionality of its store by adding the ability to not only find and purchase Android apps, but also to buy music, buy books, and rent movies. Because of this, Android Market has been renamed to Google Play. Your Galaxy Note II's user interface provides the Play Store app for accessing Google Play.

Configuring Google Wallet

Before you start buying apps in the Play Store app, you must first sign up for a Google Wallet account. If you plan to only download free apps, you do not need a Google Wallet account.

1. From a desktop computer or your Galaxy Note II, open the web browser and go to http://wallet.google.com.

2. Sign in using the Google account that you will be using to synchronize email to your Galaxy Note II. See Chapter 4, "Email," or Chapter 7, "Contacts," for information about adding a Google account to your Galaxy Note II.

3. Choose your location. If your country is not listed, you have to use free apps until it's added to the list.

4. Enter your name.

5. Enter your credit card number. This can also be a debit card that includes a Visa or MasterCard logo, also known as a check card, so that the funds actually are withdrawn from your checking account.

6. Select the month and year of the card's expiration date.

7. Enter the card's CVC number, which is also known as the security code. This is a three- or four-digit number that's printed on the back of your card.

8. Check this box if your billing address is the same as your name and home location. Otherwise, uncheck this box and enter your billing address and phone number when prompted.

9. Click Accept and Create when you finish filling in the form.

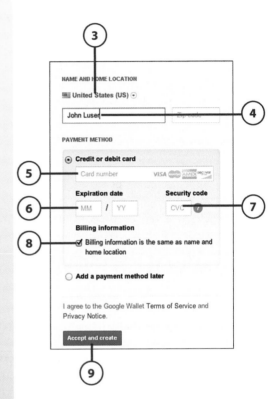

Navigating Google Play

Android is the operating system that runs your Galaxy Note II, so any apps that are made for your Galaxy Note II need to run on Android. Google Play is a place where you can search for and buy Android apps.

1. On the Home screen, touch Apps.

2. Touch the Play Store app icon.

3. Touch the Menu button to see Google Play actions.

4. Touch to see any apps you have already purchased or downloaded.

5. Touch to select which Google account you want to use when you use the Google Play store, if you have multiple Google accounts.

6. Touch to change the settings for Google Play. See the "Manage Google Play Settings" section later in this chapter for more information.

7. Touch to browse all Android apps.

8. Touch to browse all Android games.

9. Touch to search Google Play.

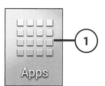

Download Free Apps

You don't have to spend money to get quality apps. Some of the best apps are actually free.

1. Touch the app you want to download.

2. Scroll down to read the app features, reviews by other people who installed it, and information on the person or company who wrote the app.

3. Scroll left and right to see the app screenshots.

4. Touch Install to download and install the app.

5. Touch to accept the app permissions and proceed with the download.

Beware of Permissions

Each time you download a free app or purchase an app from Google Play, you are prompted to accept the app permissions. App permissions are permissions the app wants to have to use features and functions on your Galaxy Note II, such as access to the wireless network or access to your phone log. Pay close attention to the kinds of permissions each app is requesting and make sure they are appropriate for the type of functionality that the app provides. For example, an app that tests network speed will likely ask for permission to access your wireless network, but if it also asks to access your list of contacts, it might mean that the app is malware and just wants to steal your contacts.

Permissions to your phone the app is requesting

Buy Apps

If an app is not free, the price is displayed next to the app icon. If you want to buy the app, remember that you need to already have a Google Wallet account. See the "Configuring Google Wallet" section earlier in the chapter for more information.

1. Touch the app you want to buy.

What If the Currency Is Different?

When you browse apps in Google Play, you might see apps that have prices in foreign currencies, such as in euros. When you purchase an app, the currency is simply converted into your local currency using the exchange rate at the time of purchase.

2. Scroll down to read the app's features, reviews by other people who have used it, and information on the person or company who created the app.

3. Scroll left and right to see the app screenshots.

4. Touch the price button or Install to download and install the app.

5. Touch to choose the means of payment.

6. Touch to purchase the app. You will receive an email from Google Play after you purchase an app. The email serves as your invoice.

Permissions to your phone the app is requesting

Manage Apps

Use the My Apps section of Google Play to update apps, delete them, or install apps that you have previously purchased.

1. Touch the Menu button.

2. Touch My Apps.

3. Touch All to see all apps that you have bought and downloaded from Google Play.

4. Look for the Installed indicator to see whether the app is currently installed.

5. Touch an app marked with Free to install a free app again. The Free readout shows a free app that you previously installed, but that is no longer installed.

6. Touch to remove an app from the list of apps.

7. Touch an app marked as Purchased to reinstall an app that you previously purchased and installed, but that is no longer installed. Because you have already purchased the app, you do not need to pay for it again.

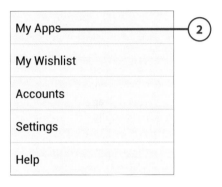

Allowing an App to Be Automatically Updated

When the developer of an app you have installed updates it to fix bugs or add new functionality, you are normally notified in the Notification bar and Notification shade so that you can manually update the app. Google Play enables you to choose to have the app automatically updated without your intervention. To do this, open the My Apps screen and touch the app you want to update automatically. Check the box labeled Allow Automatic Updating. Be aware that if these updates occur while you are on a cellular data connection, your data usage for the month will be affected.

Uninstalling an App

When you uninstall an app, you remove the app and its data from your Galaxy Note II. Although the app no longer resides on your Galaxy Note II, you can reinstall it as described in step 7 because the app remains tied to your Google account.

Touch to uninstall the app

Check to allow automatic updating

Manage Google Play Settings

1. Touch the Menu button.

2. Touch Settings.

3. Touch to enable or disable notifications of app or game updates.

4. Touch to enable or disable the setting of all apps you install to automatically update themselves.

5. Touch to enable or disable forcing all app updates to occur only when you are connected to a Wi-Fi network.

6. Touch to allow or prevent an app icon from appearing on your Home screen for each app that you install.

7. Touch to clear the Google Play search history.

8. Scroll down to see more settings.

9. Touch to adjust or set your content filtering. Use this to filter out apps, movies, music, or books that you deem to be inappropriate.

10. Touch to set a PIN that must be typed in before changing the Google Play User Control settings (Content Filtering, PIN for purchases, and Set PIN).

11. Touch to use the PIN you set in step 10 for purchasing apps, music, or books or renting movies.

12. Touch to enable or disable having AdMob ads personalized based on your interests. AdMob ads normally show up in free apps.

13. Touch to return to the main Google Play screen.

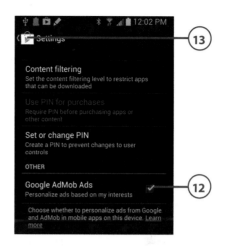

Why Lock the User Settings?

Imagine if you buy a Galaxy Note II for your child but want to make sure that he doesn't get to any undesirable content. First, you set the content filtering to restrict the content visible in Google Play. Next, you set the PIN so he can't change that setting. A similar idea goes for limiting purchases.

Accidentally Uninstall an App?

What if you accidentally uninstall an app or you uninstalled an app in the past but now decide you'd like to use it again? To get the app back, go to the My Apps view in Google Play. Scroll to that app and touch it. Touch Install to reinstall it.

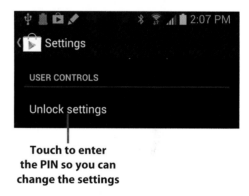

Touch to enter
the PIN so you can
change the settings

Keeping Apps Up to Date

Developers who write Android apps often update their apps to fix bugs or to add new features. With a few quick touches, it is easy for you to update the apps that you have installed.

1. If an app you have installed has an update, you see the update notification in the Notification bar.

2. Pull down the Notification bar.

3. Touch the update notification.

4. Touch one of the apps that has an update available.

5. Touch Update.

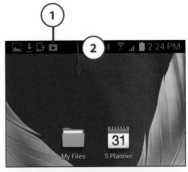

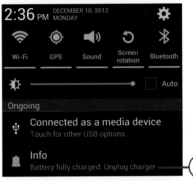

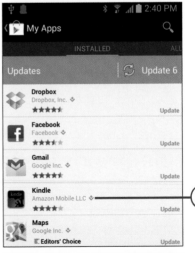

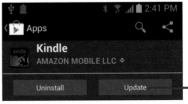

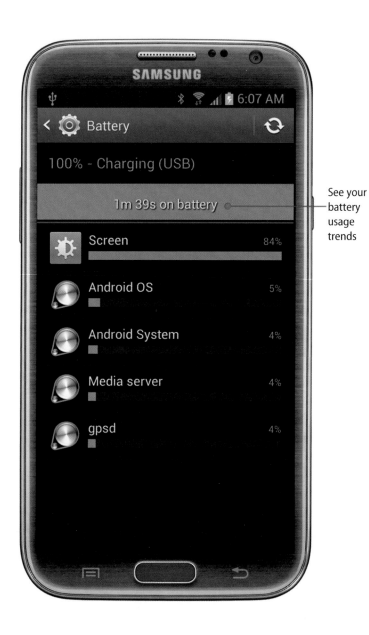

See your battery usage trends

In this chapter, you discover how to maintain your Galaxy Note II and solve problems. Topics include the following:

→ Updating Android
→ Optimizing battery life
→ Identifying battery-hungry apps
→ Caring for your Galaxy Note II

12

Maintaining Your Galaxy Note II and Solving Problems

Every so often, Google releases new versions of Android that have bug fixes and new features. In this chapter, you find out how to upgrade your Galaxy Note II to a new version of Android and how to tackle common problem-solving issues and general maintenance of your Galaxy Note II.

Updating Android

New releases of Android are always exciting because they add new features, fix bugs, and tweak the user interface. Here is how to update your Galaxy Note II.

Updating Information

Updates to Android are not on a set schedule. The update messages appear as you turn on your Galaxy Note II, and they remain in the Notification bar until you install the update. If you touch Install Later, your Galaxy Note II reminds you at short intervals—30 minutes, 1 hour, or 3 hours—that there's an update. When to install the update is up to you. You might prefer to wait to see if each new update contains any bugs that need to be worked out rather than applying each update immediately.

1. Pull down the Notification bar to open the Notification shade.

Manually Checking for Updates

If you think there should be an update for your Galaxy Note II but have not yet received the onscreen notification, you can check manually by touching Settings, About Device, and Software Update. On the Software Update screen, touch Update to check for an update.

2. Touch Software Update.

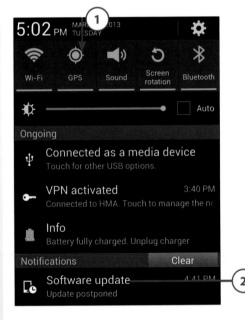

3. Touch Install in the Software Update dialog.

4. Touch OK in the next Software Update dialog. Your Galaxy Note II restarts, installs the update, and then displays the Lock screen.

Delaying an Update

If you do not want to install the software update immediately, touch Later in the Software update dialog. In the Reminder Interval dialog that appears, touch 30 Minutes, 1 Hour, or 3 Hours, as appropriate.

Touch to check manually for an update

Touch a button to delay the update for a while

Optimizing the Battery

The battery in your Galaxy Note II is a lithium-ion battery that provides good battery life as long as you take care of it. You can change the way you use your Galaxy Note II to prolong the battery life so that the battery lasts long enough for you to use the phone all day.

Carrying a Spare Battery

One of the great things about the Galaxy Note II is how easily you can remove the back and change the battery. Given this feature, you might prefer to buy and carry a spare battery instead of scrimping on display brightness and phone usage. When your current battery runs out, you can power off the Galaxy Note II, pop in the spare battery, and restart the phone in less than a minute.

Take Care of the Battery

There are specific steps you can take to take care of the battery in your Galaxy Note II and make it last longer.

Follow these steps to care for your Galaxy Note II's battery:

1. Try to avoid discharging the battery completely. Fully discharging the battery too frequently harms the battery. Instead, try to keep it partially charged at all times (except as described in the next step).

2. To avoid a false battery level indication on your Galaxy Note II, let the battery fully discharge about every 30 charges. Lithium-ion batteries do not have "memory" like older battery technologies, but fully discharging the battery once in a while helps keep the battery meter working correctly.

3. Avoid letting your Galaxy Note II get overheated because this can damage the battery and make it lose charge quickly. Do not leave your Galaxy Note II in a hot car or out in the sun anywhere, including on the beach.

4. Consider having multiple chargers. For example, you could have one at home, one at work, and one in your car. This enables you to always keep your phone charged.

Monitor Battery Use

Android enables you to see exactly what apps and system processes are using the battery on your Galaxy Note II. Armed with this information, you can alter your usage patterns to extend the Galaxy Note II's runtime on the battery.

1. On the Apps screen, touch Settings.

2. Touch Battery.

3. Touch to manually refresh the display.

4. Touch an app or Android service to see more details about it, including how much time it has been active, how much processor (CPU) time it has used, and—if the app has used data—how much data it has sent and received.

5. Touch the battery graph for more details.

6. Look at the Mobile Network Signal readout to see when the mobile network signal was being used during the battery graph's time span.

7. Look at the GPS On readout to determine when the GPS radio was being used during the battery graph's time span.

8. Look at the Wi-Fi readout to see when the Wi-Fi radio was being used during the battery graph's time span.

9. Look at the Awake readout to learn when your Galaxy Note II was awake during the battery graph's time span.

10. Look at the Screen On readout to check when your Galaxy Note II's screen was on during the battery graph's time span.

11. Look at the Charging readout to find out when your Galaxy Note II was charging during the battery graph's time span.

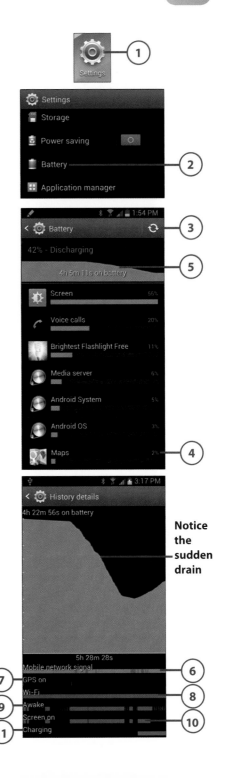

Notice the sudden drain

How Can Seeing Battery Drain Help?

If you look at the way your battery has been draining, you can see when the battery was draining the fastest, and you should be able to remember what apps you were using at that time or what you were doing on your Galaxy Note II. Based on that, you can change your usage habits—for example, you can plan to charge your Galaxy Note II after a session of phone calls. You can uninstall any apps that appear to be power hogs, or you can simply avoid using them when running on the battery.

Choose Power-Saving Options

Your Galaxy Note II includes a feature called Power Saving that enables you to reduce the amount of power it consumes. After choosing which of four power-saving options to use, you can turn Power Saving on and off by using its switch on the Settings screen.

1. Touch Settings on the Apps screen.

2. Touch the main part of the Power Saving button—anywhere apart from the switch.

3. Move the Power Saving switch to On to make the settings available.

4. Check CPU Power Saving to throttle back the processor when the Galaxy Note II is running on battery power.

5. Check Screen Power Saving to reduce the screen's brightness on the battery.

6. Check Background Color to decrease the brightness of the background when you are using email and browsing the Internet.

7. Check Turn Off Haptic Feedback to turn off vibration when you touch the screen.

8. Touch Learn About Power Saving to see tips on saving power.

9. Touch to return to the Settings screen, where you can turn Power Saving on and off by moving the Power Saving switch.

Apps and Memory

Each app you run on your Galaxy Note II has to share the phone's memory. Although Android usually does a good job of managing this memory, sometimes you have to step in to close an app that has grown too large.

1. On the Apps screen, touch Settings.

2. Touch Application Manager.

3. Touch Running to see only apps that are currently running.

4. The graph shows how much memory is being used by running apps and cached processes, and how much is free.

5. Touch an app to see more information about it.

6. Touch Stop if you believe the app is misbehaving.

7. Touch to report an app to Google. You might want to do this if it is misbehaving, using up too many resources, or you suspect it of stealing data.

8. Look at this readout to see the processes that are being used by this app.

When Should You Manually Stop an App?

After you have been using your Galaxy Note II for a while, you'll become familiar with how long it takes to do certain tasks, such as typing, navigating menus, and so on. If you notice your phone becoming slow or not behaving the way you think it should, the culprit could be a new app you recently installed. Because Android never quits an app on its own, that new app continues running in the background, which might cause your Galaxy Note II to slow down. When this happens, it is useful to manually stop an app.

Reining in Your Data Usage

If you are worried that you might exceed your data plan in a month, you can set a usage limit on your Galaxy Note II. You can even prevent apps from using data while they are running in the background.

1. On the Apps screen, touch Settings.

2. Touch Data Usage.

3. Make sure Mobile Data is checked to enable data transfer over your Galaxy Note II's cellular connection.

4. Touch to enable or disable mobile data limits. When this is enabled, your Galaxy Note II automatically cuts off all mobile data usage when the limit you set in step 6 is reached.

5. Touch to set the monthly billing cycle your cellular carrier uses for your Galaxy Note II's account.

6. Slide up and down to select the mobile data limit you want to impose. This might or might not match your cellular data plan limit.

7. Slide up and down to set a data usage warning threshold. When you reach or pass this threshold, you see a warning in the Notification bar.

8. Scroll down if necessary, and touch an app to see more details about its data usage and to control how it uses data in the background.

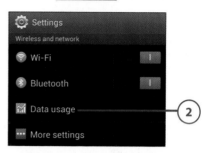

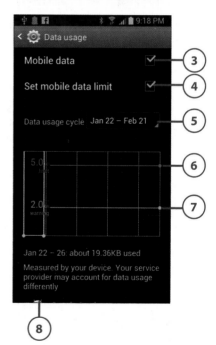

Set Background Data Limits

When you touch an app to see its data usage, you can also limit its usage when it is in the background. An app is in the background when you have launched the app but you are not currently using it. An app in the background still takes up memory and might still be transferring data.

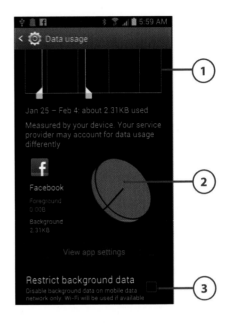

1. Look at the Data Usage chart to see the data usage for this app specifically.

2. Look at the pie chart to see the breakdown of data usage in the foreground and background.

3. Touch to restrict the app from using data while it is in the background.

Caring for the Galaxy Note II's Exterior

Because you need to touch your Galaxy Note II's screen to use it, it picks up oils and other residue from your hands. You also might get dirt on other parts of the phone. Here is how to clean your Galaxy Note II and how to avoid damaging its micro-USB port.

1. Wipe the screen with a microfiber cloth. You can purchase these in most electronic stores, or you can use the one that came with your sunglasses.

2. To clean dirt off other parts of your phone, wipe it with a damp cloth. Never use soap or chemicals on your Galaxy Note II as they can damage it.

3. When inserting the Micro-USB connector, try not to force it in the wrong way. If you damage the pins inside your Galaxy Note II, you will need to take the battery out and use an external charger to charge it.

Protecting Your Galaxy Note II's Exterior

Another way to care for your Galaxy Note II's exterior is to protect it with a case. Many different types of cases are available from both brick-and-mortar stores and online stores. To protect the screen, you can apply a screen protector. When choosing a screen protector, make sure it is thin enough for the S Pen to work effectively.

Getting Help with Your Galaxy Note II

There are many resources on the Internet where you can get help with your Galaxy Note II.

1. Visit Samsung's official Galaxy Note II site at www.samsung.com/global/microsite/galaxynote/note2/.

2. Visit Google's official Android website at www.android.com.

3. Check out Android blogs such as these:

    • Android Central at www.androidcentral.com/

    • Android Guys at www.androidguys.com/

    • Androinica at http://androinica.com/

Index

CHECK OUT MUST-HAVE BOOKS IN THE BESTSELLING MY. . . SERIES

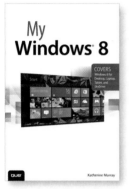

ISBN 13: 9780789749482   ISBN 13: 9780789750754   ISBN 13: 9780789749895   ISBN 13: 9780789750020

Full-Color, Step-by-Step Guides

The "My..." series is a visually rich, task-based series to help you get up and running with your new device and technology, and tap into some of the hidden, or less obvious, features. The organized, task-based format allows you to quickly and easily find exactly the task you want to accomplish, and then shows you how to achieve it with minimal text and plenty of visual cues.

Visit quepublishing.com/mybooks to learn more about the My... book series from Que.

quepublishing.com

Your purchase of *My Samsung Galaxy Note™ II* includes access to a free online edition for 45 days through the **Safari Books Online** subscription service. Nearly every Que book is available online through **Safari Books Online**, along with thousands of books and videos from publishers such as Addison-Wesley Professional, Cisco Press, Exam Cram, IBM Press, O'Reilly Media, Prentice Hall, Sams, and VMware Press.

Safari Books Online is a digital library providing searchable, on-demand access to thousands of technology, digital media, and professional development books and videos from leading publishers. With one monthly or yearly subscription price, you get unlimited access to learning tools and information on topics including mobile app and software development, tips and tricks on using your favorite gadgets, networking, project management, graphic design, and much more.

Activate your FREE Online Edition at
informit.com/safarifree

STEP 1:   Enter the coupon code: WRXBNXA.

STEP 2:   New Safari users, complete the brief registration form.
           Safari subscribers, just log in.

If you have difficulty registering on Safari or accessing the online edition,
please e-mail customer-service@safaribooksonline.com